REAL PHILOSOPHY FOR REAL PEOPLE

ROBERT McTEIGUE, S.J.

Real Philosophy for Real People

Tools for Truthful Living

IGNATIUS PRESS   SAN FRANCISCO

Ignatius Press thanks Southern Illinois Universtiy Press for permission to use an epigraph from Paul Weiss' *Modes of Being* (1958).

Excerpt from *The Return of the King* by J.R.R. Tolkien. Copyright © 1955, 1965, 1966 by J.R.R. Tolkien, renewed 1983 by Christopher R. Tolkien, John F.R. Tolkien, and Priscilla M.A.R. Tolkien; and renewed 1993, 1994 by Christopher R. Tolkien, John F.R. Tolkien, and Priscilla M.A.R. Tolkien. Reprinted by permission of Houghton Mifflin Harcourt Publishing Company. All rights reserved.

Cover art:
© iStockPhoto.com/chictype

Cover design by Enrique J. Aguilar

A SYLLOGISM OF EPIGRAPHS

Philosophers let theories get in the way of what they and everyone else know.

—Paul Weiss

It's one thing not to see the forest for the trees, but then to go on to deny the reality of the forest is a more serious matter.

—Paul Weiss

In short, the case for a sort of general guidance from the start is to be found in the fact that the road is beset with traps and temptations to the loss of liberty. There are not only pitfalls, but bottomless pits; there are not only mazes, but mazes without a centre. That is why I, for one, believe in the philosophy of providing a map of the road, with all the blind alleys and broken roads marked on it from the first. But that is not in order that men should not be free to walk the roads, but rather that they should walk on the roads on which they will remain free. And until this distinction is understood the modern debate about authority and liberty will not have ended, for it will not even have begun.

—G. K. Chesterton

To Paul Weiss, 1901–2002
He was for me a philosopher, a scholar, a teacher,
a mentor, a friend, and a father.

CONTENTS

A PARABLE

AL E. QUIS and FRED are engaged in conversation.

FRED: "If you punctured your foot on a rusty nail, what would you do?"

AL: "I would go to a doctor and get a tetanus shot."

FRED: "Are you sure?"

AL: "Yes, of course, everyone knows that's what you do."

FRED: "And if you got a paper cut, would you clean the wound with alcohol or with mud?"

AL: "With alcohol, of course! Everyone knows that. It's obvious!"

FRED: "Yes, yes it is. At least it is now ..." (Fred winks.)

FRED: "And if you wanted to lose twenty-five pounds as quickly as possible?"

AL: "Well, that depends ..."

FRED: "So it would seem. Every week, the magazine rack at the supermarket is loaded with publications promising the amazing new discovery of this or that wonder diet based on grapefruit or carrot juice or cottage cheese or aromatherapy or *something*."

AL: "What's your point?"

FRED: "Why aren't the magazine racks at the supermarket filled weekly with publications announcing the great new discovery that tetanus can be treated with grapefruit or carrot juice or cottage cheese or aromatherapy or *something*? Why don't these magazines announce on a weekly basis the amazing new discovery that paper cuts should be cleansed with rain water or motor oil or powdered laven-der or *something*?"

AL: "That's crazy. How to prevent tetanus and how to clean a cut are settled questions. The answers to those questions are well established."

FRED: "Yes, indeed. And how many diets have been touted in the last twenty years as the best, most reliable, fastest acting, foolproof diet?"

AL: "Too many to count."

FRED: "Indeed. And when you go to the supermarket and you see this week's announcement of the latest diet, do you pay close attention?"

AL: "Not at all."

FRED: "Why not?"

AL: "Because diets announced in tabloids sold in super-markets have a pitiable track record. If grapefruit mixed with catnip and dog food really was the basis for the per-fect quick weight-loss diet, then that fact would become as established and well known as the prevention of tetanus or the cleansing of a wound."

FRED: "Quite right. Now, in the past twenty *centuries*, how many philosophy texts have offered theories as the best, most reliable, and final account of a sound and livable morality? Is the number greater than the number of tabloid diets proffered in the past twenty years?"

AL: "Yes, the number would be much greater, I would imagine."

FRED: "Ah. And yet you turn to these philosophy texts, which, on your own account, have a worse track record than tabloid diet suggestions, for wisdom about how to guide your life and how to discern right from wrong (terms for which most texts cannot even agree on a com-mon definition). If any one of them really had truth with a capital 'T', wouldn't the other texts just fade away, as dangerous as alternative methods for preventing tetanus or as laughable as the latest fad diet? If you won't waste your time reading tabloid diets available in the super-market, why do you waste your time reading philosophy texts about morality? Surely, if the 'TRUTH' about right and wrong were something to be discovered and known, it would have been discovered by now. Purveyors of phil-osophical texts are just as much hucksters as purveyors of fad diets, and those who read such texts are as gullible as those who follow the fad diets. But those who read phil-osophical texts about morality are even more pitiable than desperate dieters."

AL: "How can that be?"

FRED: "It is not contrary to reason that someone might find a most or even more reliable way to lose weight quickly. But the attempt to formulate a consistent moral theory is contrary to reason. Moral theories cannot be coherent and cannot be lived because they involve too many irreconcilable antinomies."

AL: "For example?"

FRED: "How about these? Physical/non-physical; ratio-nal/nonrational; public/private; objective/subjective; law/freedom; duty/love; habit/spontaneity; principle/praxis; fact/value; absolute/relative. How can these be recon-ciled? And even if they could, in some *theoretical* way, be reconciled, how could such a moral theory be *livable*?"

AL: "Are you saying that morality is meaningless?"

FRED: "Certainly *philosophical* accounts of morality, in light of the antinomies I've just listed, are meaningless. The history of philosophical moral reflection is a collec-tion of quaint and embarrassing conceits. A systematic, coherent account of the moral life just can't be achieved.

If you want guidance in morality, just ask yourself before acting, 'What is the loving thing to do?' That is about as reliable as any other attempt at a moral theory, and it is a lot more concise."

How should Al respond to Fred?

PREFACE

Learning to Live with *Solertia*

Consider this conversation between a father and son:

SON: Dad, what's the best way to avoid making bad decisions?
FATHER: Experience.
SON: What's the best way to get experience?
FATHER: Making bad decisions.

Do you agree with the father here? Is there really any way of knowing what is good and right in this life, aside from trial and error? How can we know what to do and when to do it and the way to do it? This mysterious but real human faculty is what we call prudence, which Father William Saunders dubs "the 'mother' of all virtues". Through prudence, "a person recognizes his moral duty and the good means to accomplish it." And as Saunders points out, this virtue has three layers:

> To prudently examine a situation and then to determine a course of action, one must keep in mind three aspects of prudence: *memoria*, *docilitas* and *solertia*. *Memoria* simply means having a "true-to-being" memory which contains real things and events as they really are now and were in the past. Everyone must learn from his past experiences. Remembering what is to be done or avoided from past

experiences helps to alert us to the occasions and causes of sin, to prevent us from making the same mistakes twice and to inspire us to do what is good. Be on guard: the falsification or denial of recollection is a grave impediment to exercising prudence.

Docilitas means that a person must have docility, an open-mindedness, which makes the person receptive to the advice and counsel of other people. A person should always seek and heed the wise counsel of those who are older, more experienced and more knowledgeable.

Finally, the exercise of prudence involves *solertia*, which is sagacity. Here a person has a clear vision of the situation at hand, foresees the goal and consequences of an action, considers the special circumstances involved and overcomes the temptation of injustice, cowardice, or intemperance. With *solertia*, a person acts in a timely manner but with due reflection and consideration to decide what is good and how to do the good. With a well-formed conscience attuned to God's truth, and with the proper exercise of *memoria*, *docilitas* and *solertia*, a person will act prudently.[1]

We will return to this threefold structure of prudence at the end the preface.

The meaning of human flourishing has been disputed since humans began disputing. What does it mean to live well? What is the good life—for an individual, for a community, for society as a whole? Whatever else human flourishing might mean,[2] it must surely include the

---

[1] William Saunders, "Prudence: Mother of All Virtues", Catholic Education Resource Center, visited January 27, 2020, http://www.catholiceducation.org /en/culture/catholic-contributions/prudence-mother-of-all-virtues.html.

[2] I should say here that I am not an agnostic about what human flourishing means. In fact, I will offer some quite detailed specifics about what human flourishing does and must mean, but for now I wish to avoid tipping my hand.

following prerequisites: (1) being aware of what we must know; (2) being aware of what we cannot not know;[3] (3) being aware of what our intellectual and moral options are; (4) choosing wisely among our options; (5) acting in a manner that is consistent with what we know to be true and good.

Surely, it would be undesirable to come to know only by chance the prerequisites for human flourishing. The father's proposition of "making bad decisions to get experience to make good decisions" is a frightfully hazardous process. Likewise, it must be undesirable to arrive at the prerequisites of human flourishing by a sheer act of an unguided and unaccountable will—the raw power of choice. I say this fully aware that the United States Supreme Court disagrees with me on this matter. Justice Kennedy, in his opinion on the case *Planned Parenthood v. Casey*, famously wrote: "At the heart of liberty is the right to define one's own concept of existence, of meaning, of the universe, and of the mystery of human life."[4] But surely, a healthy and humane civilization cannot be built if its inhabitants are simply a conglomeration of willful, alienated, and inscrutably motivated units declaring for themselves (and by implication, wittingly or not, for all others) the meaning of "life, the universe, and everything".[5] Does Justice Kennedy think that no one ever wonders whether one account or another of human life or meaning is better or truer than any other? Does Justice Kennedy think that such wondering is illegitimate, dishonest, or somehow undemocratic (i.e., betraying "the heart of liberty")? Must we all stand idly by while some individuals

---

[3] See Budziszewski's *What We Can't Not Know: A Guide* (San Francisco: Ignatius Press, 2011) for a fine reflection on undeniable elements of morality.

[4] Planned Parenthood of Southeastern Pa. v. Casey, 505 U.S. 833 (1992).

[5] With a nod in the direction of Douglas Adams and his *Hitchhiker's Guide to the Galaxy* (New York: Del Rey, 1997).

or groups wreak havoc on humanity as they seek to implement the fondest wishes of their idiosyncratic concept of existence, of meaning, of the universe, and of the mystery of human life? No—that way leads to chaos and madness. If existence, meaning, the universe, and the mystery of human life are not to be insipid, tedious, and burdensome incoherencies, then there must be some way of knowing and living well, a way of knowing and living that leads to human flourishing for the human individual and the human community. One purpose of this book is to provide the reader with at least the minimum of what he needs to know in order to be able think and act humanly well, for himself and with and for others.

The world we now live in is a mess, both intellectually and morally. There seems to be little on which we can all agree. There seems to be even less available to guide us to flourishing as human individuals or a human community; there seem to be few or no resources available for leading us out of our factions or our private isolations toward a common understanding of what constitutes human nature and identity, human opportunities and obligations, human possibilities and prohibitions. My Italian grandfather, the late Guido Formisano, used to lament, "Io parlo e parlo e nessuno mi capisce" (I talk and I talk, and no one understands me). Illustrations of this dynamic are easily found. Just watch any televised political "debate", read side-by-side conflicting accounts of the work of Planned Parenthood, attend a university faculty meeting involving members from more than one department, watch videos of invited speakers at college campuses being pelted with food by unhappy students. Imagine a whole world wherein the only thing people can say about themselves and at each other is "I talk and I talk, and no one understands me." If we cannot find the

prerequisites for individual and communal human flourishing, then Guido's lament is hard to improve upon for
accuracy or to move beyond in its tragic poignancy.

To one familiar with the history of philosophy,
especially philosophy in the modern[6] and postmodern
modes,[7] it seems awfully unlikely that philosophy has
much to offer anyone who wishes to identify the necessary requirements and resources available for securing
a foundation that will allow us to build a moral house
in which we would want to live. The forms of philosophy that are most common today seem to have little to
contribute to a project of human flourishing. The problem, my mentor Paul Weiss told me frequently, is that
"philosophers let theories get in the way of what they
and everybody else know." In other words, philosophers
generate theories that deny how humans actually live and
reject what humans evidently know. There are professional philosophers who deny nonarbitrary morality yet
expect universities to honor their contracts; they question the existence of any reality outside the mind yet
correct the waiter when he brings the wrong order; they
spurn tradition but demand tenure.

Paul Weiss used to tell a story to illustrate the irony and
madness of such an approach to philosophy: "An explorer
came back from a safari in Africa. He told his friends of
how he had been trapped in the jungle by wild animals.
'There I was, with tigers in front of me and tigers behind

---

[6] For a clear account of the distinctive features of modern thought, see
Étienne Gilson's *The Unity of Philosophical Experience* (San Francisco: Ignatius
Press, 1999).

[7] For a clear account of the distinctive features of postmodern thought, see
*The Death of Truth: What's Wrong with Multiculturalism, the Rejection of Reason,
and the New Postmodern Diversity*, ed. Dennis McCallum (Minneapolis, Minn.:
Bethany House, 1996).

me, lions to the right of me and lions to the left of me.' His friends asked him, 'What did you do?' The explorer replied, 'What *could* I do? I was killed!'"

Like the explorer who lived to tell the story of his own death, many philosophers write and teach and love and make plans and raise children and cash checks, all the while assuring others how unsure we in fact must be about what can be known or what ought to be done. I say that philosophy can do better than that; hence the title of this book, "Real Philosophy for Real People". I maintain that human reason (carefully exercised), informed by the human heart (properly formed), can know a great deal about what it means to be human and what it means to succeed or fail as a human individual and as a human community.

While saying this, I am conscious that I do not want to write yet another volume in the long line of philosophical works that claim to have the absolute, final, and irreformable answers about all-of-everything. I do not want to write a book that will be advertised as "the last and only book you will ever need!" No, my intent is much more modest, much more realistic, and, if I may say so, both more attainable and more desirable. My intent is to put together a set of philosophical tools to help one to know what one should know and to do what one should do and to face challenges and contradictions when and as they occur. Across the miles and the years, I have met, heard of, and read about many people who say something like this: "I read/saw/heard something the other day, and it seemed to me not right. But I could not quite put my finger on why it was not right." If you have had that experience, then this book is for you. Perhaps ambitiously, I also hope that the set of philosophical tools I am assembling is "portable", akin to what I have described to my students as a "philosophical Swiss army knife". In other words, I want to avoid developing a ponderous and unwieldy philosophical system that is so elaborate and cumbersome that one must have a mystic's insight and a savant's memory before making or evaluating moral claims or assertions of truth.

Instead, I want to assemble a set of philosophical tools that may be seen to be so intuitively interconnected and easily usable that, once understood, they can be used readily, whether one is in the classroom or in the pub, in the church or in the home, on the shop floor or on the floor of the senate. I am confident that this project is possible and the tools are effective because I have been teaching students how to assemble and use such philosophical tools for years. By the use of simple diagrams and with reference to some classic texts and concepts, I have been able to help my students to achieve an admirable degree of philosophical sophistication in a relatively brief period of time. What my students and I have done in the classroom, I hope to be able to do now for the readers of this book.

Having said that, let's have another look at that difficult-to-define word *solertia* before going forward with our plans to put it to good use. Surrounded by a flurry of conflicting claims and assertions, some of which will do each and all of us grave harm if left unchecked, we have to be able to sort out the nature and lethality of ideas presented to us. On this view, philosophy is a very high-stakes activity for individuals, communities, and even civilizations. It is not an exercise for armchair thinkers to be undertaken at whim or at leisure. Philosophy is not a verbal form of Sudoku puzzles. Ideas, as Richard Weaver observed decades ago, have consequences. That is why we have to stay philosophically alert. The ready transition from alertness to action is the work of *solertia*. *Solertia* is like the IFF ("Identify: Friend-or-Foe") program of a combat aircraft. Once something shows up on your radar screen, so to speak, it is within striking distance. The combat pilot needs to know immediately if what is coming toward him intends him weal or woe. One of the overarching purposes of this book is to give the reader the foundation for developing the habit of *solertia*, to avoid being unwittingly poisoned, infected, or assassinated by bad ideas and dishonest claims. Toward that end, I would like to reflect further on Saunders' comments on the virtue of prudence, emphasizing why the cultivation of *solertia* is an essential task in every age, but especially in ours. Among other things, this book can be understood as an outline of the knowledge and skills necessary to cultivate and exercise *solertia* well.

An illustration may help. While it has long been observed since the time of ancient Greece that philosophy is the product of leisure—that is, a good done for its own sake and not for the gain of something else—it is not a discipline undertaken to alleviate the tedium of otherwise empty hours. It is not the work of those who simply have too much time on their hands or who do not suffer the necessity of getting "a real job". Likewise, it is not a luxury but, rather, is a necessity for individuals, communities, and cultures seeking to secure truth and resist error. When I was studying theology in London, I lamented to a German classmate that while I was glad to be able to read great books, I was frustrated because it seemed that we were receiving no guidance in taking the words off the page and bringing them to life in our lives. He looked at me in horror and gasped, "But if we depart from the text, we will engage in *speculation*!" As we continued to talk, I gathered that he saw the work of a scholar to be primarily that of a curator of texts and concepts, an intellectual archaeologist who gathers fragments from the distant past, dusts them off, and puts them on display behind a glass case so that they can be admired. That approach to the intellectual vocation, I have observed, if left to its own devices, becomes a desiccated quibbling over minutiae, neither giving life to human life nor light to human searching. I believe that we need more and can do better than that. My intention is to use this book to support that claim.

Using Saunders as a point of departure, I hope to show that we can (and, indeed, we need to) live a rational and moral life guided by thinkers who show us how to be more fully human and fully alive. We can and we ought to foster a mode of philosophy that facilitates knowing that which is highest and also knowing that which is most human so that we can see, teach, and achieve what is highest for humans. To do so, we must refer to and learn from the texts of the Western intellectual tradition and, at the same time, be ready, willing, and able to take those texts into the ordinary and extraordinary of daily life.

Memoria allows us to draw upon the past, our own and that of our forebears, to recall the cautionary tales, the shining examples, the aspirations, and the exhortations needed to guide us, our thinking, and our behavior within our present and into our future. In the development of the teaching that became this book, I have learned from great thinkers living and dead, from noble characters I have read of or have met, and from the brightness and darkness of the human heart that I have observed in myself and in others. What I call "real philosophy for real people" is not the product of philosophical spontaneous combustion, a full-blown theory arising from nothing and nowhere, the product of what an old friend called the results of "data-free analysis".[8] Rather, it is a fresh synthesis of a long and noble tradition of human reflection and experience, expressed

[8] William Sneck, S.J.

in a way that people can hear, evaluate, and apply today. I have made (I hope good) use of *memoria* in the writing of this book. My intention was to write it in such a way that readers could easily remember and put to use what I have written here.

The use of *memoria* here is aptly summarized by Peter Kreeft: "This book is not just me. It's 90 per cent unoriginal. That is what makes it different. Those tiresome and shallow modern books that all say the same thing are too desperately striving to be original. In every area of life the secret of originality is to stop trying to be original and just tell the truth as you see it."[9] Making use of *memoria* in this fashion, what I call real philosophy for real people is my attempt to tell the truth as I see it. I know that I stand upon the shoulders of giants. I also know that I am limited and fallible. Consequently, I will not be surprised when others identify limits or even errors in what I have proposed here—I am willing to be corrected; indeed, I welcome correction because correction is an aid to finding the truth that liberates. I am also sure that much of what I write here has been put to the test and found worthy in the age-old crucible of human experience and reflection. In addition, I can state that what I have written here has been battle-tested and battle-hardened by being put to work in the university classroom year after year. I invite the reader to be the judge of whether what is written here points to truth, goodness, and human dignity in an intelligible and livable manner. I call upon the reader to accept the challenge of being a thinker who is at once critical and sympathetic, one ready, willing, and able to give this work a fair hearing. What I wish for most is a reader with the imagination and generosity to put to the test in his

---

[9] Peter Kreeft, *Angels (and Demons): What Do We Really Know about Them?* (San Francisco: Ignatius Press, 1995), p. 27.

own life what is written here. To do that, a reader must be ready not only with *memoria* but with the second aspect of prudence, that of *docilitas*, to which we now turn.

Docilitas is the etymological root of the English words "docile" and "docility". In common parlance, "docile" connotes passivity, submissiveness, and being easily led, like a sheep. In that light, it seems scarcely credible that *docilitas* could be praiseworthy. Docility seems to be a characteristic cultivated among the witless masses by some nefarious Orwellian regime.

To the contrary, *docilitas*, as noted by Saunders, is an open-mindedness, a readiness to learn. Proper docility requires an openness to humility, properly understood. Humility is rooted in the truth; it is a willingness to tell the truth about oneself, even if that truth is painful. A properly humble person is open to the painful truth that he might be in error; that humility frees him from the worst forms of dogmatism and self-righteousness. Proper humility is the rich soil in which true docility can grow. A humble and docile person loves and seeks the truth; he is ready to admit fallibility and be corrected (humility) and is willing to be taught (docility).

Saint Thomas Aquinas said, "Now the reason why the philosopher is compared to the poet is that both are concerned with wonders. For the myths with which the poets deal are composed of wonders, and the philosophers themselves were moved to philosophize as a result of wonder. And since wonder stems from ignorance, they were obviously moved to philosophize in order to escape from ignorance."[10] The reward of cultivating proper docility and

---

[10] Saint Thomas Aquinas, *Commentary on Aristotle's Metaphysics*, trans. John Rowan (Chicago: Henry Regnery Company, 1961), I, lesson 3, no. 55 (archive .org/details/AquinasCommentaryOnTheMetaphysics/page/n47).

humility is the delight of being amazed by new truths (i.e., to be "concerned with wonders"), deeper understanding, and the discovery of unexpected goodness and beauty. Cast in those terms, the task of real philosophy for real people becomes a great adventure. Armed with a desire for truth and value, equipped with intellectual tools (the philosophical Swiss army knife), an honest and ordinarily intelligent person can set off confidently on a delightful and amazing (if often arduous) path, able to discern true from false, good from evil, the humane from the dehumanizing. How could any sane person *not* desire *docilitas*?

It remains to consider *solertia*, an aspect of prudence that is not easily defined. It might be rendered in French as *savoir-faire*. In colloquial English, it might be understood to be "know-how" joined with the ability "to think on one's feet". A colleague who once described herself as "just an old hillbilly woman from Arkansas" (who happened to have doctorates in biology and moral theology) praised those who have what she called "good ol' walkin' around sense". That could also be another way of understanding *solertia*.

More graphically, when I think of *solertia*, I think of Richard Marcinko's account of how he taught a team of Special Forces operators of the Navy SEALS how to shoot.[11] He said that when one first learns how to shoot, one begins by learning how to zero in on the target and then to project fire toward that target. Over time, one learns how to zero in on the target and then to fire at it with (one hopes) greater degrees of consistent and timely accuracy. Because of the extraordinary demands and dangers faced by the SEALS, Marcinko put his team through

[11] Richard Marcinko, *Rogue Warrior* (New York: Pocket Books, 1992), pp. 222–23.

constant, vigorous practice, intending to form them so that they could take the actions of "acquire" (the target) and *then* "fire" and combine them into the *one* action of "acquire-fire".

The cultivation of *solertia* may be understood analogously to Marcinko's training of his SEAL team in marksmanship. One must be so well trained to identify philosophical challenges, so steeped in solid understandings of right knowing and right action, that even when one is faced with an unexpected moral claim or assertion of truth, one is readily, objectively, creatively, confidently, and resolutely able to respond. Be sure that such an ability is not inborn and does not happen by accident. One needs both the understanding born of sound education and the habits of heart and action that come from well-guided moral formation. Speaking of military conflict, there is the old adage, "In combat, one does not rise to the occasion; one falls to the level of one's training." Absent a deeply ingrained intellectual and moral habituation, we will not have available the *solertia* needed to respond to the many and unpredictable intellectual and moral challenges that will inevitably come our way. As I have so often told my students, "Be prepared—or be surprised." The project of real philosophy for real people is to provide the honest thinker with the intellectual preparation needed for a cultivation of *solertia*, without which one will surely be cognitively confounded by those who are in error but who do not know it or morally mugged by those who would do us ill, even if they are well-intentioned.

There is a social benefit to the cultivation of *solertia*. When others who are less certain of the grounds of truth or goodness, or who are fearful of moral or intellectual conflict, see that one can readily and honestly meet challenges with a quick mind and discerning heart, they might gain hope that they, too, can face the unexpected without undue fear and without compromising *memoria* or *docilitas*. That is why I am convinced that the project of real philosophy for real people can be a benefit for both the human individual and the human community.

If you have read this far, I suspect that you are ready to go forward as a philosopher on the move, as one seeking more of truth and goodness, unwilling to dismiss the truths of the past or be unduly bound by its errors, keen to face the future with an open mind and a discerning heart, and eager to travel with companions who wish to join in the humane and humanizing venture of building a moral house in which we would want to live. If you wish to go forward in this necessary venture, then I expect that you are not naïve and that you will not be surprised that your own weakness and limits and those of others, including people who are fearful or who are opposed to the human liberation brought about by truth and goodness, may all array themselves against you. Be prepared or be surprised. Let's begin!

CHAPTER 1

THINKING AND LIVING
HUMANLY WELL

There are many philosophical truths to be obtained....
We cannot escape the task by claiming to be modest. We
are, to be sure, finite, bewildered and far from omniscient.
But unless we try to live up to the ideal of having a sound,
universal knowledge, we are bound to be entangled in
a tissue of preconceptions and prejudices. We do not
achieve modesty by refusing to ask after the real nature
of things. That is but a device for riding on the crest of
current beliefs and preparing our ideas for passage into the
limbo of historic errors. True modesty demands a coura-
geous attempt to express systematically, in intelligible language, truths that are at least faintly discernible to a child.[1]

We have a problem. We are surrounded by people
who do not understand what they are doing or why they
do what they do. We are surrounded by people and by
the panoply of media making claims about what is true or
false or praiseworthy or blameworthy; at the same time,
we are surrounded by (often the same) people and various media making claims that nothing could be true or
false or praiseworthy or blameworthy. There are people

---

[1] Paul Weiss, *Nature and Man* (New York: Henry Holt, 1947), p. xxii.

who seem unduly confident in their assertions; there are people glad to tell you that no one knows anything and that therefore no one can tell anyone else what is good or bad, true or false; there are people who call upon you to spend time, money, and energy on this or that thing, person, or idea if you wish to be happy; there are people who urge you to spend time, money, and energy on this or that thing, person, or idea to distract you from the awful truth that no person or thing or idea can ever make you happy. In short, we are flooded with claims about reality, humanity, and morality, and there seems to be little evidence that we might find a means of getting clear of the flood swirling around us and arriving at sure conclusions about such urgent essentials as meaning, purpose, and value.

For millennia, men have asked, in one form or another, philosopher Immanuel Kant's three great questions: "What can I know?... What should I do?... What may I hope?"[2] Theologians, mystics, atheists, agnostics, philosophers, artists, scientists, academics, laborers, and countless others have, in the spoken and written word and in every form of art, struggled with those questions, formulated excessively modest or cautiously tentative or assuredly irreformable answers, and have proposed reasons for hope or despair based upon what they saw to be known or unknowable about what is true or false, good or evil. In our own time, we have seen all manner of universities, churches, statesmen, and spokesmen espousing every imaginable theory and anti-theory, every imaginable account of the uniqueness or banality of human life, every imaginable account of what is or is not morally forbidden, required, or indifferent.

---

[2] Immanuel Kant, *Critique of Pure Reason*, trans. and ed. Paul Guyer and Allen W. Wood (Cambridge: Cambridge University Press, 1998), p. 677.

Education, whether in school, home, place of worship, or workplace—wherever men are—does take place, variously forming, informing, transforming, deforming, and misinforming, whether the pupils are aware or unaware of the pedagogical processes at work.

Most people do not have the time, energy, ability, or inclination to sort through the competing voices, ideologies, or enthusiasms that tout the answers or non-answers that are being advocated or denigrated. At the same time, every person has, at least occasionally, a desire to be sure about what can or cannot be known about the real, the human, and the good. And every person, without exception, wittingly or unwittingly, depends upon a network of (compatible or incompatible) assumptions about the real, the human, and the good. And every person, without exception, is surrounded by people who have their own set of tested and untested networks of assumptions. How can we talk with one another, how can we argue and come to agreement or identify irreconcilable differences, how can we live together well, when it seems that we are each lost in our own private network of claims and assertions of what it means to be a human person living in the world?

In this chapter, we will begin our project of coming to clarity about the real, the human, and the good. We will lay the foundation for developing a coherent and persuasive account of how to answer Kant's three great questions. We will also begin to develop a set of tools we can use to identify and understand (and perhaps correct or benefit from) the network of moral claims and assertions of truth from those around us. With these goals in mind, let's start by reflecting on the nature of education. If our project succeeds, we will have made great progress in developing a guide for thinking and living *humanly* well.

Range of Education

Public	Formal	
		Degrees and diplomas
		Exams and grades
		Classroom discourse
		Students as peers
		Discourse outside classroom: Students as friends
		Discourse outside classroom: Student with intimate friend
		Individual student alone with conscience and God
Private	Informal	

Consider the two parallel continua of the diagram above. One line extends from the most public to the most private; the second line extends from the most formal to the most informal. Let's draw a series of lines across the continua, starting at the levels of the most public and most formal, and progress down to the most private and the most informal.

At the top of the continua, we have education at the most public and most formal levels. What is education like at this level? Here we find degrees, certificates, diplomas. A community of academicians, through the conferral of a degree and the production of a diploma, publicly certifies that the recipient has attained a certain level of knowledge and skill within a given discipline. The student in question is presented as having earned that recognition along with the rights and privileges concomitant with the public and formal certification.

Moving down the continua, we are at a slightly less public and formal level. Here we are at the level of examinations and grades. At this level, an individual academic evaluates and certifies the level of knowledge and skill of a student within the academic's area of competence. The criteria for the evaluation and the record of the evaluation are public and formal but are not displayed as publicly as a diploma or as formally conferred as a degree.

Moving farther down, we are near the midpoint between public/private, formal/informal. This point represents education as it takes place in the classroom. In the classroom, there is an academic specialist and a group of students lacking the instructor's credentials and knowledge and seeking credentials and (one hopes) knowledge of their own. The discourse within a classroom is still formal, insofar as it is not an undirected conversation about just anything; yet it is not as fixed and formal as the conferral of a degree. The discourse is often one-sided, with the instructor as the primary or even sole speaker, with the expectation that the role of the students is to digest what is offered. In the classroom, especially if the class is run as a seminar, the discourse is more conversational, that is, more likely open to spontaneity, creativity, alteration, and error.

Conversational discourse within the classroom is more formal than conversation outside the classroom. The former conversation is structured around the purposes of the course in which the student is enrolled. The conversation is usually guided by the instructor, who holds the speakers to standards of evidence and argument that are essential to the purposes of the classroom but would more likely be unwelcome (and often unnecessary) in a less formal setting outside of the classroom.

The discourse within a classroom is still rather public. It takes place in a space designed for a form of instruction that is set apart for that purpose. The students have a responsibility to understand and remember what the instructor has said in the classroom and will be held accountable for the understanding/remembering when a public/formal examination is administered.

Moving down the continua again, we move toward the more informal and the more private. What I have in mind here is a group of students talking among themselves outside of the classroom, say, in a study session preparing for an exam. The discourse at this level is not freewheeling; the students have met to address topics relevant to the aims of the course in which they are enrolled. Their conversation is not led by a paid authority who governs/guides students. The students are more or less peers, with no one formally identified as an authority whose office is to guide their conversation. They talk amongst themselves, but with less structure and rigor than what is expected of them within the professor's classroom.

At this point on the continua, we have entered the predominantly private and informal levels. Here we might find students, gathered together more as friends than as students, talking about course content but in a more colloquial and personal way. The conversation is likely to have a more affective rather than rational tonality; the students are more likely to talk about how the course content impinges upon their lives, stirring up, for example, enthusiasm, indifference, or disgust, etc. The standards of evidence and argument are considerably lower here, and there is more of an emphasis on exploration of ideas and expression of opinions rather than on a more rigorous attempt to prove or disprove.

Tending toward the bottom of the continua, here we might find one student/friend speaking to another, but with a level of intimacy not found at the previous levels. For example, here one might say, "What the professor said about morality was painful for me, because it reminded me of something that I am ashamed of, something I've never told anyone about ..." The conversation partners might well apply course content to this conversation, but the emphasis is on them as individuals being affected by course content, rather than on course content itself.

At the bottom of the continua, we are at the level of the most private and the most informal. Here an individual, sitting alone with his conscience, reflects upon, evaluates, accepts or rejects or modifies what he has been taught. Here, he seeks livable answers to the questions that trouble him. His deliberations are known only to him and those intimates to whom he wishes to reveal them. A student might also acknowledge that God is attending upon these ruminations.

Why is an understanding of the levels of education important? I maintain that a sound education reaches a student at all of the levels of the two continua. I can justify my claim by illustrating what results from the compartmentalization of the levels from each other.

Imagine a medical student who passes all his examinations, earns his degree, and is a master of medical skills and knowledge—so far, so good. If his education provides him only with information and makes no effort at forming his character at the deeper, informal/private levels, he will be a highly competent, morally dangerous doctor. He will be, at best, an amoral technician armed with a scalpel and a prescription pad. He will not be able to identify readily the ultimate purposes and moral limits and obligations of his work as a doctor. Who would want to be the patient of such a doctor?

Now imagine a medical student who is virtuous, honorable, and compassionate. He also has poor study skills, cannot memorize the names of bones or medicines or organs, and cannot learn to wield a scalpel properly. Who would encourage him to continue with his medical studies?

In light of this example as an illustration of the previous diagram, we can see that a sound education must impart knowledge and skill, must encourage conversation among colleagues and among friends, and must form character as well. Allow me a digression on character: Moral character, the generally stable orientation of the moral agent relative to the good, is a product of the intersection of the habits of mind, affections, and practice. The formation of character, relative to the parallel continua of education, may be influenced by all the levels of the continua. The expression of character, initiated from the most private level of the continua, may be expressed or revealed along the whole length of the continua.

Any education that does not address well the public/ private, formal/informal dimensions, that does not form character and community, that does not foster competence and humility, fails to address the needs of both the human individual and the human community.

We might sum up the matter this way: A proper education will seek to inform, to form, and to transform. Of course, we would expect an education to inform—to impart knowledge. A proper education will also form— that is, actualize heretofore untapped potential. The best education will also transform—that is, correct what is in error and improve what could be better.

Here is a real-life illustration of what troubles me about inadequate education: I was driving in northeast Pennsylvania one summer, shortly after the time when most colleges have finished the academic year and graduation ceremonies are behind them. Along the road, a local college (I forget the name) had erected a billboard that read:

"The Graduates of Other Schools Get Degrees—*Our* Graduates Get *Jobs.*" Well, okay—as someone who has had at various times degrees with no job and at various other times degrees with a job, I can say confidently that having a degree with a job is obviously more desirable than having degrees with no job. However, for an institute of higher learning to suggest (as this college did with the billboards) that the success or failure of an education is measured precisely by no standard other than that of employment is dehumanizing and therefore irrational. Such a view of education sees human persons primarily as public, economic units and the primary (if not sole) goal of education as employment. This view of the human person as primarily mercantile is unworthy of human dignity, as we shall see in later chapters.

For an education to be worthy of the human person, the human community, and the flourishing of both, it must span the entire spectrum illustrated by the above parallel continua, which describe what the range of a sound education entails. With this *scope* of a sound education in mind, let's turn now to consider a *method* for putting to critical use what such an education can offer.

We have all been involved in arguments, discussions, and disputes. Often these encounters lead to frustration rather than fruition. Very often we are confident that our position is sound and our assertions are true, but we cannot seem to articulate *why* what we hold is sound and true. Likewise, we may deeply suspect that what another says is doubtful or wrong or perhaps even despicable— but again, we cannot quite seem to articulate *why* we suspect that the other party is in error. We find ourselves, with others, in a tangle of claims and counterclaims, assertions and assumptions. Very often, we find the conversation jumping from one topic to another as evidence and argument are hurled back and forth. No progress is made, and eventually we throw up our hands in exasperation, and, if we are polite, we might suggest to others that the best we can do is to "agree to disagree". While that apparently polite termination of discussion may be tempting, especially since it seems to be less painful than banging one's head against a conversational brick wall, that inclination to "agree to disagree" can stem from and even encourage lazy and sloppy thinking. That inclination can corrode individual, communal, and cultural commitment to finding truth. It unjustly severs us from the obligation to hold ourselves and others accountable for the claims that are made. It can appear to absolve us from any duty to know what is truly real, human, and good. Granted, there are topics about which honorable people may disagree, but those topics are actually rarer than the "dictatorship of relativism"[3] would have us believe.

One reason I have chosen to undertake the writing of this book is that I fear that today we are too readily inclined to give up on using contested conversation as a means toward arriving at truth. I think that we should be most reluctant to give up on efforts to find a true resolution of differences. Even if we can articulate our position only imperfectly, even if we can justify our moral claims and our assertions of truth only provisionally, let us, in the words of Paul Weiss, "at least make an effort that is worthy of a refutation." Let's pay truth, humanity, goodness, and our interlocutors the compliment of our best efforts rather than settling for offering them a shrug of the shoulders and the tacit, polite, but often facile admission of failure known as "agreeing to disagree".

---

[3] Joseph Ratzinger, Homily, Mass *Pro Eligendo Summo Pontifice*, May 18, 2005.

The difficulty we face in making progress in our disputes is that the features of the real, the human, and the good are complex and profoundly intertwined. As I often tell my students, "If you pull on the thread, you get the whole rug." In other words, claims about what is real, human, and good are always interrelated and bring along with them, for better or worse, whether known to their advocates or not, an enormous amount of philosophical "baggage". A claim about morality, for example, always entails an accompanying anthropology (here understood as an account of human nature) and an accompanying metaphysics (here understood as an account of what is ultimately real).

Fortunately (as we shall see later), the ways in which the various elements of reality, humanity, and morality can be coherently connected and livable in practice are relatively few in number. For now, however, we must ascertain a method of thinking through the affirmations/denials that we make and the affirmations/denials we encounter about the real, the human, and the good, so that we can identify for ourselves and others precisely where and why so many assertions of truth and moral claims go wrong. Most people do not know that whenever they make a claim, they are (wittingly or not) endorsing a "package", i.e., an interconnected set of metaphysics, anthropology, and ethics. Many people, I have found, do not know (or if they suspect, they very often cannot articulate) the scope of the assumptions, implications, grounds, and bounds of their assertions. The investigative method I will propose here will help you and your conversation partners to make explicit the reach and connections that always are in play whenever an assertion or claim is made. This method I have called "Thinking in Four Directions".

Thinking in Four Directions

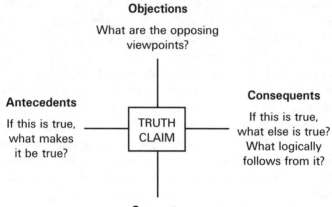

Objections

What are the opposing
viewpoints?

Antecedents

If this is true,
what makes
it be true?

TRUTH
CLAIM

Consequents

If this is true,
what else is true?
What logically
follows from it?

Supports

What supports the claim?

This method requires one to think extensively and intensively. Thinking extensively, as one can see from the diagram, enables one to see the reach or range of the claim being evaluated, as one considers the scope of what the claim entails, in terms of its antecedents and consequents, its support and objections. Thinking intensively, one can begin to see the interconnections between metaphysics, anthropology, and ethics ingredients in a claim.[4] Thinking extensively along the Four Directions and thinking intensively along the connections of ethics, anthropology, and metaphysics, one can begin to see the whole package entailed by and undergirding each claim, thereby allowing one to evaluate the package as a whole. This method affords one a systematic, thorough, and reliable means for making clear what the acceptance or rejection of a moral

[4] We will reflect in greater detail about the meaning of thinking intensively later in this chapter.

claim or assertion of truth demands. That alone makes it valuable for one who would know the truth and live accordingly. At the same time, the method of thinking extensively and intensively gives one the means to identify for one's conversation partner the package being endorsed (often unwittingly) that is concomitant with the claim or assertion being made by that speaker. If your conversation partner is willing to learn, he might actually be glad when you point out that the package he is endorsing is in fact intellectually untenable, at odds with reality, and morally indefensible. If the conversation partner is an ideologue and is merely arguing a case rather than searching for the truth and striving to live in harmony with the truth, then at least observers of your dispute can see, with your help, the errors being advocated by your opponent. Let's turn now to each of the points of the Four Directions.

On the left side of the diagram we see the antecedents that underlie the claim or assertion to be evaluated. For now, I will simply lay out the process and give a concrete example shortly. The antecedents answer the question, "If Proposition X is true, what makes it be true?" Said another way: The antecedents address the question, "What are the conditions of possibility that must obtain in order for Proposition X to be true?" In other words, for a claimant to assert the truth of Proposition X, he (at least) implicitly maintains that all of the proposition's antecedents are true. When he asserts that Proposition X is true, he has in effect "bought" the package that includes all of the antecedents that undergird his claim. If he is not willing to accept the truth of *all* of X's antecedents, then logic demands that he withdraw his support of Proposition X. (Whether we should expect every claimant to be logical is another question, a painful one in fact, which we will address later in the book.)

On the right side of the diagram, we see the consequents—all that follows logically from the truth or falsity of Proposition X. The consequents address these questions: "If this claim is true, what follows from it? What else is true? What does it require/prohibit? What else are you now allowed to say about reality because this is true?" Like its relationship to its antecedents, the relationship of Proposition X to its consequents constitutes a package. An endorsement of Proposition X necessarily entails an (at least implicit) endorsement of all of its consequents on the part of the advocate of the proposition. In asserting the truth of X, the claimant has "bought" the package of its consequents, whether he knows it or not, whether he likes it or not. If he is not willing to accept the truth of *all* of X's consequents, then logic demands that he withdraw his support of Proposition X.

In fact, we must make an even broader statement. When a claimant asserts the truth of Proposition X, then he must, in order to be coherent, endorse all of the antecedents *and* all of the consequents associated with the proposition. In other words, one who endorses the truth of a proposition buys a much bigger package than most people realize. Intellectual honesty and rigor demand that we begin by looking at our own claims, our own endorsements, and begin to map out the packages of antecedents-consequents and metaphysics/anthropology/ethics that we have been purchasing. Such a venture of self-scrutiny is an important exercise in humility. If we take such a trek, we may find that ideas long cherished have also been ill considered. Such a venture also holds great promise, as it might confirm the foundations of our ideas and allow us to discover new opportunities to put our ideas to work in unexpected ways.

Let's take a look at a simple, real-life illustration of how attention to antecedents-consequents and moral claims/truth assertions as a package can be a useful pedagogical device. A few years ago, I was contacted by a teacher of an eighth-grade class. The teacher was dismayed to discover that the majority of her students had a view of human freedom that equated freedom with license. In other words, "real freedom" = "I get to do whatever I want, and no one may tell me otherwise." Admittedly, it should not be surprising that young adolescents should have such an adolescent view of freedom. Nonetheless, that view of freedom, left uncorrected, could easily lead to disaster in their lives later on. The teacher invited me to address her class and to speak to them about freedom. I was reluctant to speak to a group so young because I have taught almost exclusively in the university classroom.

When I entered her classroom, I observed that two girls sitting in the front row were wearing eyeglasses. I asked to examine their glasses. They complied and handed me their glasses. I waved their eyeglasses in the air and announced to the class: "These glasses are mine now. I am using my freedom to declare them mine. I have not 'stolen' them; I have merely relocated them. Given your definition of freedom, I know you will not insist on calling my action of relocation 'stealing', as you would then be imposing your definition of morality on me, thereby limiting my freedom, an action from which your definition of freedom protects me."

Turning to the girls whose eyeglasses I now firmly held, I said: "Ladies, I outweigh the two of you put together, so if you try forcibly to relocate your eyeglasses from my hands to yours, I will use my freedom to smack you down." The students sat in stunned silence. I then asked: "Do you want to live in a world wherein this sort of thing will happen to you every day for the rest of your lives?" They assured me that they did not. "That may be so—but, that is the world that you bought when you endorsed that definition of freedom." Immediately, they said, "Then we want to find a better definition of freedom!" Once they were able to see the erroneous and dangerous package that they had bought, they were able to see quickly that they wanted and needed and deserved a much better package.

Moral claims and assertions of truth are never free-floating; they do not exist in a vacuum. Claims and assertions, especially the most important ones, come with a long history of reflection and contention. Intellectual honesty and rigor demand that we investigate and apply to our propositions supporting and contrary analysis and evidence. To do otherwise indicates that we are sloppy and lazy thinkers. If we comb through ancillary argumentation, merely looking for talking points and clever sound bites to support our prior commitments, then we are not honest thinkers, and surely not philosophers, but rather cranks and ideologues more suited for blogs, television news, and "debates" on Facebook.

At the lower portion of the diagram we see "supports". These include data, arguments, expert opinions, human experience, reflections on history, etc., that concur with the proposition. At the upper portion of the diagram are "objections". These include contrary evidence, arguments, alternative points of view, etc. One way to ascertain how seriously one should take a claimant and his propositions is to ascertain how familiar he is with *both* supports and objections. We can see that Saint Thomas Aquinas is a role model for this fearlessly honest and fair quality of disputation. In his *Summa Theologica*, he always began the treatment of a disputed question by presenting the best arguments of his opponents *first*.

Now let's get a bit more specific and prepare for an example of Thinking in Four Directions in relation to a moral claim. Let's say we encounter the proposition "X is morally good and praiseworthy." How shall we apply the Four Directions to such a proposition? We will begin with the antecedents.

The antecedents of a moral claim would include at the least the following: metaphysics, anthropology, and ethics. Let's look at each of these in turn.

Metaphysics is an attempt at a systematic, comprehensive account of what is first and final, of what constitutes reality, of what is ultimate. If one's account of the real is that reality is illusory (as might be seen in certain forms of Buddhism, for example), then it does not make much sense to be asserting that any moral claim is *true*.

Anthropology (undergirded by a compatible metaphysics—a topic we will consider at length later on) is an account of what a human person is, of how a human person is like or unlike other kinds of beings. If one's anthropology is purely biological, and man is nothing but an animal, then a moral claim assigning praise to delay of gratification or to a painful sacrifice would make no sense.

Ethics (undergirded by a compatible metaphysics *and* anthropology—a topic we will consider at length later on) offers an account of what is good and evil, how we may know what is good and evil, how and why we ought to do good and avoid evil. If one's moral methodology can yield only idiosyncratic preferences (e.g., "Loyalty is good", "Loyalty makes me feel good", and "I like anchovies on pizza" are not significantly different statements), then one cannot rationally assert that "All men are always and everywhere obliged to be loyal."

Now let's look at a moral claim in relation to its consequents. If moral Proposition X is true, then what follows from that fact, both logically and morally? In other words, what obligations does X impose? What prohibitions does X impose? Which matters, in light of X, must be judged as morally neutral, morally irrelevant, or morally opaque?

Which moral doors are opened or closed because Proposition X is true?

In evaluating moral Proposition X, careful attention must be paid to supports and objections. Are there confirming or contrary expert opinions? Has this proposition been dealt with by philosophers, theologians, historians, artists, etc.? Are there data that buttress or diminish the credibility of Proposition X?

I am the first to admit that the methodology of Thinking in Four Directions is a demanding, sometimes time-consuming exercise. Nonetheless, I commend it to the reader because it is a reliable path to reaching clarity and truth; it is a safeguard against fallacy and sophistry. It encourages audacity, because it takes for granted that the truth can be found and is worth the effort; it encourages humility, for it demands that one be as ready to be corrected as one is to be found correct.

Let's review where we are and ascertain what we need to do next. We live in a world wherein we are surrounded by competing and often incompatible claims of truth and falsehood, good and evil. We have seen that accounts of the real, the human, and the good are tightly interwoven in complex packages that must be evaluated. We have examined a methodology that allows us to locate and evaluate claims and assertions within the complex contexts in which they reside—bounded by antecedents, consequents, supports, and objections. This method of Thinking in Four Directions affords us an opportunity to see more clearly the tacit assumptions, (often) overlooked implications, and range of evidence that must be acknowledged if one is to evaluate well a moral claim or an assertion of truth and then act in harmony with what has been shown to be true and good. Searching for what is true and good, and acting in harmony with what one knows to be true and good, is, I maintain, distinctively human and particularly humanizing. We fail at being human if we do not search rightly and act truly—hence the title of this chapter: "Thinking and Living Humanly Well."

Earlier in this chapter, I spoke of thinking "extensively", i.e., looking at the range of a proposition's reach or scope. Thinking in Four Directions helps us to think extensively. I also mentioned the need to think "intensively". When I speak to my students about the need to think intensively, I use the image of "drilling down" into a proposition, to get to its "bottom". I also speak of the need to pivot at the foundation of a proposition and return to it, armed with the better understanding that a proposition requires in order to be held firmly and reliably as true or false, good or evil. In order to help my students understand what I mean by thinking intensively or drilling down into a proposition, I offer the students a diagram of what I call the "Ethical Wedding Cake" (hereafter referred to as "EWC"). I will review it in some detail now because it is the central theme of this book. When my mentor, the late Paul Weiss, introduced in class a central theme of one of his works-in-progress, he said: "If I'm right—here's where I'm right; and if I'm wrong— here's where I'm wrong." I make a similar claim about the EWC. The rest of the book stands or falls upon the EWC. I urge the reader to examine what follows, with its accompanying diagrams, with a sympathetic yet critical eye.

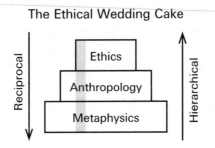

The Ethical Wedding Cake

To understand and evaluate this diagram properly, let's have a quick review of terms and then focus on the interrelations among the layers, which constitute the most important aspect of the diagram.

Metaphysics is the discipline that investigates the real as such and strives to offer a systematic, comprehensive account of the real as such. It addresses such questions as: What are the ingredients of the real? What is the nature of time? What is the relationship between the real and time? What is the origin of the real? What is the purpose of the real? Why is there something rather than nothing? Metaphysics is at the bottom of the diagram because all other disciplines are, in one form or another, applied specifications of metaphysics. Metaphysics is the foundational discipline upon which the other disciplines are built.

Anthropology is the discipline that investigates the nature of the human person. It addresses such questions as: What makes a human person distinctively human? Is a human person anything other than his body? If so, what is that and what is its relationship to the body? Are there rational elements of human nature? Are there nonrational[5] elements of human nature? What are the conditions for the possibility of distinctively human interaction? Note in the diagram above the relation between metaphysics and anthropology. Anthropology is depicted as narrower than metaphysics because there are aspects of the real that are not properly human; so understood, anthropology can be seen as one specialization of the real, but not all of the real, because some of the real is not human at all.

Ethics as a discipline is the science and art of evaluating human behavior in terms of ought and ought not. It is a

[5] *Non*rational, not *ir*rational. We will reflect on that distinction at length in the chapter on anthropology.

science (in the classical sense of *scientia*) insofar as it is a systematic body of knowledge based on deductions from principles. It is an art insofar as it fosters a creative application of principle, based on intuition, experience, and imagination. It addresses such questions as: What is good? What is evil? How can we know right from wrong? What is the nature of law, obligation, sanction, prohibition, duty, conscience, virtue, vice? How can one live a praiseworthy life? Why live a praiseworthy life? Note in the diagram above the relation between anthropology and ethics. Ethics is depicted as narrower than anthropology because human nature is more than just the moral dimension of human life.

With these definitions, more detailed than previously seen in this chapter, clearly in mind, let's look at the interrelations among the disciplines, as depicted in the diagram of the EWC. I will use a somewhat jocular but nonetheless revealing illustration to make my case for how these disciplines are related. We will start at the top, with ethics, and then "drill" our way down through anthropology to metaphysics. At metaphysics, we will pivot and make our way back up to ethics, armed with a clarity and insight we would not have had unless we had made the journey from ethics through anthropology and metaphysics and back again.

In 1985, when I was just out of graduate school for the first time, a popular music video on MTV was David Lee Roth's version of a song made popular by Louis Armstrong back in the early 1930s, "Just a Gigolo". I applied my philosopher's eye to what Mr. Roth presented on the screen during his music video. I did not like what I saw. I decided to put Mr. Roth to the test and give his video a philosopher's evaluation. What follows are the results of my analysis.

In the video, Roth cavorts with scantily clad, apparently heavily siliconized, glassy-eyed female models who seemed to delight in submitting themselves to his gyrations and ogling. "The moral of Roth's story", I would recount to my classes years later, "is that the zenith of human experience is the friction-induced release of endorphins, obtained by rubbing oneself against slabs of warm and pliable flesh also known as 'women'."

Then I would ask my students, "If the account of ethics embedded in this video is correct, what are the antecedents and consequents? Which moral doors open or close if Roth's ethics is correct? Is Mr. Roth an honorable man? What is it about the human and the real that could make David Lee Roth and his music video praiseworthy?"

Now I would ask my students to join me in "drilling down" from Roth's ethics (i.e., that which is supremely, if not solely, good is physical pleasure obtained by using women as instruments) to the anthropology that is *logically entailed* (whether Roth knows it or not) by his ethics. In the world of Roth's music video, anthropology is reduced to the lowest form of biology. Human persons are simply animal receptors of sensory stimuli. More graphically, I would tell my students that, "In Roth's anthropology, human persons are simply bags of nerve endings and appetites waiting to be tickled and fed." If that anthropology is in fact true, then what kind of metaphysics does that anthropology *logically entail*? In other words, what sort of account of the real *must* be true in order to undergird such an anthropology rightly?

As a metaphysician, David Lee Roth, in order to be consistent with the ethics that he has (at least implicitly) endorsed in his music video, along with the required and supporting anthropology that his ethics requires, must be a metaphysical materialist. In other words, the only thing that is real, the only thing that matters, is matter. Bodies, of one type or another, comprise all of reality.

Mr. Roth, almost certainly unwittingly, in presenting through his video a certain form of human interaction as desirable, good, and praiseworthy, bought a package comprising a hedonist ethics, a physical reductionist anthropology, and a materialist metaphysics.[6] Let's retrace our steps through his EWC and see if we can find some alternatives he overlooked and did not consider.

What if, having drilled down to metaphysics from his ethics, Socrates said something like this: "Wait a minute! What if materialism is not a sound metaphysical account of the real? What if there can be something real that transcends matter?"[7] If reality includes that which is nonmaterial, then, at the level of anthropology, man-as-merely-biological would not be the only option available to Mr. Roth. It might be legitimate to consider an account of the human that has a nonmaterial principle—a soul, for example. If a plausible account of human nature could include a nonmaterial principle, then a base form of hedonism need not be the only ethics to be considered. If venereal pleasure is not the summit of human life, then perhaps David Lee Roth's music video "Just a Gigolo" might not be a merely entertaining depiction of human life but, rather, a debasing of human life.

Let us grant, for now, that I have not yet made the case for metaphysical transcendence or a nonmaterial human principle or for a moral methodology beyond advocating the primacy of sensual pleasure. Presently, I have only shown the relationships among the antecedents of Roth's

[6] These terms, "hedonist", "physical reductionist", and "materialist", will be defined more precisely in later chapters.

[7] I will make a case in the chapter on metaphysics that materialism is not an adequate account of the real.

production of this music video, as well as the change in consequents if alternatives to the antecedents are offered. My point here is not to hold up David Lee Roth for censure. My intention is to use him and that particular video to show that the apparently rarefied, philosophical abstractions of the interrelations between metaphysics, anthropology, and ethics can be identified and evaluated even in the mundane, banal, and flippant (but still philosophically significant) context of a music video on MTV. In fact, the dynamic interplay of those three disciplines is found wherever there is morally significant human behavior. Consequently, we would do well to reflect further on the relationships among them.

With this illustration in mind, we can better understand the relations that exist between layers of the EWC. From the bottom up, the relations between them are hierarchical—that is, a relation of natural rank. On this view, metaphysics is the primary discipline, allowing other disciplines to emerge that are specifications of metaphysics. If metaphysics is the study of reality-as-such, then anthropology is the study of reality-as-human, and ethics is the study of human-reality-as-moral.

In turn, the metaphysics endorsed will work for certain kinds of anthropology and not others. For example, if you insist that reality is only material and subject to decay, then metaphysics precludes the possibility of an anthropology that allows for an immaterial, immortal soul. Likewise, an anthropology that insists that humans are nothing but moral animals precludes an ethics that idealizes sacrificial love of God and neighbor.

Moving from the top down, the relationship among the layers is reciprocal. That is, an upper layer requires or entails support from a particular kind of foundation and not others. For example, an ethics extolling base pleasure as the highest good could not be supported by an anthropology that includes the immortality of the human soul. Similarly, such an anthropology cannot be supported by a metaphysics that precludes immaterial reality.

Ethical Wedding Cake

Coherent and Incoherent Relations among the Layers

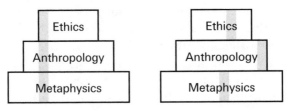

I tell my students repeatedly that the most important element to understand regarding the EWC is the relationship between the layers. A moral claim is incoherent unless the layers representing them are in proper alignment. A moral claim requires a certain anthropology and metaphysics and precludes others. In other words, a certain type of moral claim demands and logically entails a properly corresponding anthropology and a corresponding metaphysics to undergird them all. We can see in this diagram a depiction of a coherent (not necessarily true) account of the relationships between the layers of a given ethics, anthropology, and metaphysics. Apart from this form of right relation, a moral claim is incoherent. As we saw in the Roth example, a moral claim accounted for by a base form of hedonism can only be supported by a solely physical anthropology that requires a materialist metaphysics. If the advocate of a moral claim is unwilling to endorse the anthropology and metaphysics that his ethics requires, then he has eliminated himself from the conversation as a meaningful speaker; he is unwilling to engage in, and perhaps incapable of, the serious and demanding exertions required of one who would wish the kind of examined life that Socrates said is the only life worth living.

In the diagram above, we see depicted the conflicted and invalid relations among the layers of the EWC in an incoherent moral claim. The layers are out of alignment. In this arrangement, we might have a moral claim grounded upon a base form of hedonism, "supported" by an anthropology that includes an immortal soul and "supported" by a materialist metaphysics. With a right understanding of the EWC and the relations among the layers, one can point out to a claimant that his "justification" of his moral claim is incoherent. An honest man will make the necessary adjustments (with or without gratitude or enthusiasm); a lazy man or a dishonest man will not—thereby revealing himself to be a fool at best and a charlatan at worst.

Let's review and sum up what we have accomplished in this chapter before moving on to chapter 2. We have observed that we live in a swirl of assertions of truth, moral claims, and their attendant underlying theories and concomitant implications. We have seen that we need a clear-eyed understanding and a rigorous methodology to free us from the tangle of competing voices demanding our assent, or at least our acquiescent silence. We have seen that learning to think extensively (i.e., Thinking in Four Directions) and learning to think intensively (i.e., attending to the interrelations of the layers of the EWC) enable us to identify flaws, inconsistencies, and incoherencies in thought and practice. The habits of thinking extensively and intensively can free us from distraction and illusion; those same habits benefit us by demanding of us a high but attainable degree of intellectual and moral rigor and clarity.

Granted, by the end of this book, we will not have solved all philosophical problems; we will not have satisfied all intellectual and moral disputants. I maintain, and hope to show by the end of this work, that we *can* cut through the morass and dissolve a great deal of confusion. I say this because I have found that, despite the apparent plethora of assertions, claims, and theories, the actual number of possibilities for the interrelations of metaphysics, anthropology, and ethics is in fact surprisingly small. My purpose here is to outline a taxonomy of these three disciplines and to show that their untenable forms and the incoherent relations that may obtain among them are quite readily identifiable. I will also go on to show that a lucid, practical account of assertions of truth and moral claims is not beyond the reach of an ordinarily intelligent person. My intention is to offer a robust philosophy that is worthy of confidence, easily correctable, and in fact livable.

Before I attempt to deliver what I have just promised, I must take two more preliminary steps. In chapter 2, I will address the contentious issue of the relationship between faith and reason. In attempting to account for the real, the human, and the good, men of goodwill have had recourse to the resources of philosophy and theology—two disciplines that history has shown are often apparently and sometimes truly at odds with one another. My account will be incomplete if I do not address the encounter between faith and reason and identify the resources available to those who would seek to offer a systematic account of the real, the human, and the good.

I have claimed in this chapter that one test of a philosophy is whether or not it is livable. If one is to have a livable philosophy, as I understand it, then questions such as the following must be addressed: What must the world look like, and how does one live in it, if one endorses this or that package of metaphysics, anthropology, and ethics rather than another? If we commit to Thinking in Four Directions, how shall we live? These are important questions for many reasons. For the moment, I will address just one reason: an (implicitly or explicitly) endorsed package I will call a "world view". If we can survey a catalogue of possible world views, we can see clearly (if imperfectly) the import of choosing one package over another. We want a world view that grounds a world in which we can live humanly well. We also want to be clear about what an inhuman world view looks like, so we can be on guard against it. Chapter 3, addressing a taxonomy of world views, will allow us to see painted in broad strokes the range of helps or harms that come to us should we endorse or reject a given package of metaphysics, anthropology, and ethics.

Coming to the habit of thinking extensively and intensively, aware of the offerings of faith and reason, alert to the pitfalls and promises of distinctive world views, we will be in a position to begin a survey of better and worse answers to Kant's three questions: "What can I know? What should I do? What may I hope?"

CHAPTER 2

FAITH AND REASON— WHO NEEDS THEM?

Faith and reason are like two wings on which the human spirit rises to the contemplation of truth; and God has placed in the human heart a desire to know the truth—in a word, to know himself—so that, by knowing and loving God, men and women may also come to the fullness of truth about themselves (cf. *Ex* 33:18; *Ps* 27:8–9; 63:2–3; *Jn* 14:8; *1 Jn* 3:2).

—Pope John Paul II, *Fides et Ratio*

I approach this chapter with some trepidation. Those who wish to compartmentalize reason/philosophy from faith/theology for the sake of maintaining the intellectual rigor of the former might say, "Aha! This is where the author, a priest and a *Jesuit*, shows his true colors! He wishes to appear to be writing a work of *philosophy*, but now we see that he will devote a chapter to special pleading and sneak *theology* in through the back door. An apparent work of philosophy is in fact a work of crypto-catechism."

At the same time, those who wish to compartmentalize faith/theology from reason/philosophy for the sake of maintaining the purity of faith and the fidelity of theology from the blandishments, seductions, or perversities of the latter might say, "Aha! This is where the author, a priest

and a *Jesuit*, shows his true colors! He ostensibly allies himself with belief, but now we see that he will devote a chapter to special pleading and subordinate divine revelation to
an exclusively secular exercise of reason."

To both sets of concerned parties, I can say that the
short answer is, "No". A more thorough answer will take
a little longer to explain.

The apparent tension between faith and reason, between
philosophy and theology, has a wide reach and very deep
roots. In Plato's *Euthyphro*, we see Socrates tie the reader
in knots with the question, "Is something beloved of the
gods because it is good, or is something good because it is
beloved of the gods?" Plato seems to present a dilemma:
If the former is the case, then some reality (in this instance,
the goodness of any given thing) is superior to the gods
and they *must* love it—thereby diminishing divine freedom; if the latter is the case, then good and evil are merely
matters of divine whim, and morality is wholly arbitrary.

Robert Sokolowski summarizes the apparent tension
between philosophy and theology this way:

> Christian faith is said to be in accordance with reason and
> yet to go beyond reason. This claim immediately gives rise
> to a difficulty. On the one hand concordance of faith with
> reason seems to reduce Christian belief to rational think-
> ing and to natural human experience; on the other hand
> the difference between faith and reason seems to make
> belief unreasonable and arbitrary. The difficulty—like all
> theological difficulties—is not merely speculative. It has
> repercussions in Christian moral behavior, in education,
> and in the understanding Christians will have of their
> place in the world and in their social order.[1]

[1] Robert Sokolowski, *The God of Faith and Reason: Foundations of Christian
Theology* (Washington, D.C.: Catholic University of America Press, 1982,
1995), p. xiii.

I wish to propose a way of understanding the encounter between faith and reason that will not wither under criticisms from fideists or rationalists and that can do justice to the disciplines of philosophy and theology. With that understanding in place, we can then turn to the difficult problem of outlining a realist metaphysics that is at once robust enough to withstand philosophical scrutiny and of sufficient depth and breadth to be of service to theology. In other words, I will attempt here to depict a way of understanding and philosophizing that is open to the sapiential dimension.

Granted, "sapiential" (from the Latin *sapientia*, "wisdom") is not a word used in everyday conversation. Alas, it is not likely to be used even by most academics today. Nonetheless, the word itself points to a dimension of reality that is essential for our purposes—the dimension of wisdom. But what is wisdom? The work of wisdom is to acquire the clarity and completeness of vision necessary to see how everything might be properly understood and arranged in order to bring about the fulfillment and completion of all things, each according to its nature—that is, according to its *end* or ultimate purpose. Put another way, wisdom is the vision necessary to understand reality according to the right order of things, according to the reason, goodness, and purposes of God. In a passage on the "office of the wise man", Saint Thomas Aquinas echoes Aristotle's belief that the wise "order things rightly and govern them well", noting that a just "government" of things comes from an attention to their "end", which is always a good.[2] Wisdom flows from the truth—not just any truth, "but ... that truth which is the origin of all truth, namely, which belongs to the first principle whereby

[2] Saint Thomas Aquinas, *Summa Contra Gentiles*, trans. Anton C. Pegis (South Bend, Ind.: University of Notre Dame Press, 1975), bk. 1, chap. 1.

all things are". The philosopher's task is not only to teach and spread the truth, but "to refute opposing falsehood", much as a doctor at once promotes wellness and eliminates sickness. In this view, the sapiential dimension of philosophy (including the actual living-out of wisdom by the wise man) is that aspect of philosophy meant to bring about the right ordering (i.e., freeing from error) of all through the right ordering of mind (knowing the truth), heart (loving the truth because it is true and therefore good), and action (doing the truth—that is, arranging individual and communal life in light of God's purposes for creation). It helps us to know, love, and achieve the divine intention for creation.

With Saint Thomas' insight in mind, we can appreciate better John Paul II's desire to recover this dimension of wisdom in philosophy.

> To be consonant with the word of God, philosophy needs first of all to recover its *sapiential dimension* as a search for the ultimate and overarching meaning of life....This sapiential dimension is all the more necessary today, because the immense expansion of humanity's technical capability demands a renewed and sharpened sense of ultimate values. If this technology is not ordered to something greater than a merely utilitarian end, then it could soon prove inhuman and even become [a] potential destroyer of the human race.[3]

First, I think a nod to the skeptics is in order. With the dangers of militant fundamentalisms around the world and the banal popularity of "bumper sticker theology" (e.g., "God said it, I believe it—that settles it", "Would Jesus

---

[3] John Paul II, Encyclical Letter *Fides et Ratio*, on the Relationship between Faith and Reason (September 14, 1998), no. 81.

drive an SUV?", and "Too blessed to be distressed!") in the United States, one must respect those who are wary of fideists among the faithful. At the same time, it would be wrong to allow faith-based claims to be dismissed simply because they are faith-based claims:

> Many of the intellectuals who discuss the role of dialogue in public life have begun with the presupposition that all public discourse should be based on claims that are reasonable and publicly defensible. Of course, this has generated tremendous debate about what constitutes 'reasonableness'. Still, the prevailing view has been that religious appeals or moral claims based on religious belief are ruled out of bounds. Further, any consideration of ultimate metaphysical issues of human purpose, the meaning of life, or considerations of an afterlife are inappropriate for public discourse. In the apt phrase of Richard John Neuhaus, the cosmopolitan elite expect us to operate in a 'naked public square'. Public discourse about tax laws, building bridges, rights to expression, and individual freedoms are permitted. But it is viewed as gauche, as tacky, as out of place, to raise religious and metaphysical questions in public.[4]

What I propose here is a model for discourse between faith and philosophy that neither unduly limits nor over-extends philosophy while at the same time ensuring that faith and the faithful are not without resources in the face of the smug, peremptory *ad hominem* agnosticism of popular culture.

At the same time, one must acknowledge the legitimate concerns of those who would guard the transcendent

[4] Gregory R. Beabout, "John Paul II on Faith and Reason", in *A Celebration of the Thought of John Paul II* (St. Louis: St. Louis University Press, 1998), pp. 166–67.

character of divine revelation and religious faith. Søren Kierkegaard lamented that even in his day (150 years prior to Stephen Hawking, Richard Dawkins, and Christopher Hitchens), reason was exalted as the demanding and exacting discipline, the respectable discipline, while faith and theology were for the faint of heart and soft of head:

> After all, in the poets love has its priests, and sometimes one hears a voice which knows how to defend it; but of faith one hears never a word. Who speaks in honor of this passion? Philosophy goes further. Theology sits rouged at the window and courts its favor, offering to sell her charms to philosophy. It is supposed to be difficult to understand Hegel, but to understand Abraham is a trifle. To go beyond Hegel is a miracle, but to get beyond Abraham is the easiest thing of all.[5]

Without much difficulty (and often, alas, without other options readily available), one may find what I call the "Linear Model" of the relationship between faith and reason. Paradoxically, this model is often endorsed by ordinary (and "professional") skeptics and believers, even though it serves neither party well.

Linear Model of Faith and Reason

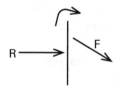

[5] Søren Kierkegaard, *Fear and Trembling*, trans. Walter Lowrie (Princeton, N.J.: Princeton University Press, 1968), p. 15.

Making use of (American) football imagery: In the quest to find answers to the great questions, reason/philosophy can carry the ball just so far. To enter the end zone, where the answers lie, one must hand off the ball to faith/theology, which brings the ball in for a touchdown. At first glance, this Linear Model appears to be incapable of offending anyone—reason does what reason does, and faith does what faith does, and no conflicts are necessary because there is no lasting contact, much less overlap, between them and, best of all, the ball ends up in the end zone. What more could anyone want?

This model, however, is deeply flawed. In the Linear Model, faith is rendered unintelligible to reason, and acts of faith can only appear as inexplicably willing suspensions of disbelief. In light of such an impoverished presentation of faith, reasonable people would be inclined to search for reality, truth, and value apart from any reference to faith at all.

At the same time, reason appears to offer faith little or no service or occasion for self-examination. Much less can faith expect such a truncated view of reason to be a resource for articulating the contents of faith to believers or unbelievers. Upon examining more closely the Linear Model, one would not be surprised to find theologians and philosophers walking away from each other, each group muttering about the other, "Why do they even bother?"

I think we can do better than the Linear Model of the relationship between faith and reason. John McDade, S.J., offers a concise and compelling account for why we should not be satisfied with either rationalism or fideism:

> I would see philosophy and theology as jointly part of the one enterprise of human beings coming to a reflection on what is open to us, and to which we are open. The truth

conferred by God's revelation is a truth to be understood
in the light of reason: the balance of that statement can be
disrupted in two ways: on the one hand, by a rationalism
which makes claims for the powers of human reason too
bold to be sustained, and on the other, by a fideism with
its distrust of reason. The first sets up the human mind
as the ultimate adjudicator of all questions, often on very
narrow foundations, and rules out, *a priori*, the possibility
of religious faith. If the mind becomes just a calculator, it
is a very deficient instrument of understanding. Fideism,
more common among religious people, rules out the critical scrutiny of religious assertions. It implies: 'Don't ask
questions, just believe,' and that too is a form of nihilism,
a counsel of despair that fails to value the gift of reason
as well as of faith. Neither position will benefit human
beings.[6]

My purpose here is not to offer an extensive account
of a proper relationship between faith and reason. For
such an account, I can recommend to the reader the many
works of Josef Pieper, among others. My purpose is much
more narrow and modest. I wish to show that it is not
illegitimate to make use of vocabulary and categories bor-
rowed from theology or philosophy. As will be seen in
chapter 5, making use of the theological themes of "mystery" and "sacrament" will be essential for grounding a
philosophically sound account of human nature. The view
of the relationship between faith and reason I will argue
for here will allow us to use theological tools for philosophical purposes without compromising the nature or
integrity of either philosophy or theology. This view of

---

[6]John McDade, S.J., "A Message from the Principal", in "Heythrop College Freshman Guide 2009", Yumpu, visited January 27, 2020, https://www
.yumpu.com/en/document/read/36444527/the-executive-committee-hey
throp-college.

the relationship between faith and reason will allow us to see that the theological categories of mystery and sacrament are both intelligible and valuable *philosophical* tools that can be deployed *without a prior assent of religious faith.*

Toward that end, what I propose here is a model of faith and reason that I call the "Intersecting Model". In this model, reason examines what faith proposes. Contrary to what some may expect, the initial question reason asks during its examination of the content of faith is not "Is it true?" but, rather, "Is it coherent or incoherent?"

Intersecting Model of Faith and Reason

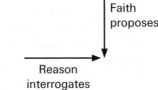

Faith
proposes

Reason
interrogates

On this view, as a result of the interrogation of faith by reason, three outcomes are possible. One possible outcome of the interrogation of faith by reason is that reason will do no more than maintain a respectful silence. This first instance I call an encounter with the *mystical*. Here, what faith proposes is so transcendent, so sublime, that reason cannot honestly offer a critical judgment. What I have in mind here, for example, is the poetry of Saint John of the Cross or the more elevated passages of the writings of Saint Teresa of Ávila.

Perhaps a more familiar and poignant illustration might be better. All can agree that the death of a child is the deepest wound that a parent can suffer. It is easy enough to imagine that one parent who has already lost a child might say to a parent who has just suffered such a loss, "I understand." But it would be horrifically wrong for a person without children to say to such grieving parents, "Oh! I know just how you feel!" I think most folks would agree that the appropriate response from one who has not suffered such a loss is a respectful silence.

A second possible result of the interrogation of faith by reason in this model is *mystery*.[7] Here, reason cannot ascertain whether what faith proposes is true or false, verifiable or falsifiable. Nonetheless, it can determine that the particular mystery of faith is not incoherent, i.e., is not nonsense, and that its meaning cannot be exhaustively known.[8] For example, Catholic faith can speak of three Persons of the Holy Trinity within one divine nature or of the two natures in the one Person of Christ. In these cases, reason can provide faith a great service by contributing reflections on the meaning of nature, person, relations, etc. The philosopher can provide guidance and encouragement for those of the faithful who are inclined to meditate further upon these mysteries and articulate them to believers and nonbelievers alike. At the same time, philosophy can show to the nonbeliever that although the mysteries of the Trinity or of Christ are not fully within the capacity of philosophy to know and define, it can show to even the most skeptical

[7] I use this word very cautiously. I remember hearing comedian George Carlin give a monologue entitled "Heavy Mysteries". He recounts some unsatisfying exchanges during Sunday School. He claims that whenever he asked a serious question, Sister would reply, "Well, it's a mystery", by which she meant (according to Carlin), "Shut up and stop thinking!" I certainly am *not* using "mystery" in that sense!

[8] This understanding of mystery will be very important in later chapters as we work out our anthropology. I will argue that the human person is a mystery; far from suggesting that the human person is unintelligible, person as mystery will be indicative of the profound value of the human individual.

that these mysteries are meaningful in themselves and are not incoherent, whether one assents to them in faith or not.

Reason, reflecting on mysteries proposed by faith, can make use of the extensive form of thinking (antecedents/consequents) referred to in chapter 1. For example, my mentor, Paul Weiss, an agnostic Jewish metaphysician, questioned me at length about various mysteries of Catholic theology, among them that of priest as *alter Christus* (another Christ) and the mystery of the Holy Eucharist. He would ask, "If this is true, what makes it be true?" (i.e., he was asking about antecedents) and "If this is true, what follows from it?" (i.e., Paul was asking about consequents). We could have long and lively conversations about these mysteries of faith, I as a believer, he as an agnostic, both of us as *philosophers*, without violating the integrity of either theology or philosophy.

The third possible outcome from this intersection of faith and reason is *understanding*. This understanding that faith offers a philosophical use of reason comes in two forms. In the first, faith proposes what philosophy may well already know and take for granted, e.g., the Golden Rule. I would call this an "understanding of confirmation"; here, faith may simply add its voice to confirm what is known by philosophy.

The second form of understanding that faith may offer philosophy, I call an "understanding of epiphany". In this case, faith discloses something that is knowable to the philosopher by unaided reason, but the concept in question would not have occurred to the philosopher without the assistance of divine revelation. Here, faith assists philosophy in its venture of discovery.

Two illustrations of this point may be useful here; one, I expect that academics may find very controversial; the

other, less so. It has been argued that the concept of creation *ex nihilo* (i.e., creation from nothing—God created
that which is other than him without making use of any
preexisting material) did not occur to the human mind
until after the infusion of the Christian revelation.[9] Once
that concept has been proposed to the human mind from
outside of the human mind, then reason can examine the
concept and find that it is a very stimulating theme worthy
of further rational examination. In later chapters, we will
take up the issue of the import of the relationship between
God as Creator *ex nihilo* and the human person as creature.

Less controversial (by which I mean not as frequently
argued about in the professional literature—so perhaps it
would be better to use the word "controverted" rather
than "controversial"), I think, would be my intention to
borrow the concept of "sacrament" from Catholic theology for philosophical purposes. Specifically, I hope to
show in the chapter on anthropology that the concept of
sacrament is a remarkably useful tool for understanding the
nature of the human person, especially the complex interactions of which a person with material and nonmaterial
dimensions is capable. I hope to show in the chapter on
anthropology that, in light of the aforementioned Intersecting Model, such a move is philosophically legitimate.

The Intersecting Model is superior to the Linear Model
in several ways. First, using the Intersecting Model's
method of interrogation, the intelligibility of faith may be
made evident by reason. Second, the integrity of faith is not
compromised, inasmuch as faith-as-mystical and faith-as-
mystery need not be dismissed as nonsense by philosophy

[9] See Sokolowski, *The God of Faith and Reason*; Kenneth Schmitz, *The Gift: Creation* (Milwaukee, Wis.: Marquette University Press, 1982); and Mortimer Adler, *How to Think about God: A Guide for the 20th Century Pagan* (New York: Macmillan, 1991).

or demythologized by overly solicitous theologians seeking philosophical respectability. Third, both faith and reason may make their unique and valuable contributions to each other. Fourth, reason is not asked to do more than it ought or can, namely, to verify or falsify that which is beyond its capacity to ascertain.

In addition, the Intersecting Model complements well the forms of interaction between faith and philosophy identified by John Paul II in *Fides et Ratio*. There, he speaks of modes or "stances" of faith to philosophy: a philosophy completely independent of the Gospel's revelation;[10] a philosophy positively influenced by faith;[11] and a philosophy that functions within theology to achieve some understanding of faith.[12] Using the Intersecting Model, philosophy may function with integrity prior to the encounter with faith; it is open to positive influence from faith; it may function within theology to advance the understanding of the content of faith.

To sum up: People of religious faith, especially Catholic Christian faith, will find the view of faith/reason, philosophy/theology advocated here to be most congenial. Nonetheless, I maintain that no religious faith is required at all to understand, evaluate, or apply the contents of this book. I took the trouble to write this chapter so as to secure for later use some theological tools that, once rationally understood, even apart from any faith commitment, may be deployed most effectively and fruitfully in the articulation of a justified and illuminating account of the nature of the human person. I suggest that the reader refer to this chapter while reading the later chapter on anthropology.

[10] *Fides et Ratio*, no. 75.
[11] Ibid., no. 76.
[12] Ibid., no. 77.

CHAPTER 3

WORLD VIEWS—WHAT THEY ARE AND WHY THEY MATTER

And I think to myself . . . what a wonderful world.

—Louis Armstrong[1]

In the previous chapter, I sought to justify the legitimacy of borrowing from theology some tools that will prove useful later on to our philosophical efforts in this book. More importantly, in the first chapter, I laid out the basic project of this book, which is to identify the relations that obtain among metaphysics, anthropology, and ethics in whatever Ethical Wedding Cake one explicitly or tacitly endorses. (The largest portion of this book will identify how various combinations of these three disciplines might cohere and be lived.) We also saw in the first chapter a methodology for philosophical investigations called "Thinking in Four Directions". What happens when we combine the Ethical Wedding Cake with the Four Directions?

In other words, how far do the antecedents and consequents of a given Ethical Wedding Cake reach? I hope to show in this chapter that their reach constitutes what I will

---

[1] "What a Wonderful World" was first recorded on August 16, 1967, in New York City by Louis Armstrong. It was composed by George David Weiss and George Douglas (a.k.a. Bob Thiele).

call here a "world view". As a philosophical concept, the term "world view" has an interesting pedigree. The term itself is a translation from the German *Weltanschauung* and was first used by Immanuel Kant. That word was used by a variety of scholars in a variety of contexts in the latter part of the nineteenth century and into the present day.

I must confess to approaching this chapter with some trepidation. In this chapter in particular, I intend to move the reader quickly through a broad sweep of history, summarizing complex ideas, texts, movements, and events in a rather terse fashion. I fully expect that at least some academic professionals will read this chapter and find some glaring fault, some unforgivable omission, some objectionable compression of detail.

I found some consolation in the words of Dennis McCallum, in his introduction to an anthology he edited that focused on introducing postmodernism to an intelligent but nonprofessorial audience. I wish to make my own his statement of intention, his admission of limitation, and his request for understanding. What he said about the challenges of introducing postmodernism I wish to say about my introduction to world views:

> Although this book was written by scholars, communicators, and researchers from several different fields, it isn't an academic book. *The Death of Truth* brings postmodernism and its impact on today's society within the reach of people who have never studied it before, in an attempt to move awareness of this school of thought out of academia and into popular discussion. Because our goal is to help the public at large grasp the magnitude of the postmodern shift, scholarly readers may not be happy with missing distinctions, apparent lack of subtleties, and even the complete absence of certain categories, terms, and authors in our discussion. We hope academic readers will agree with

us that the public should also understand, at some level, the sweeping changes going on in intellectual and professional circles and the impact of those changes on their everyday lives, and will kindly, to be colloquial, cut us some slack. We expect that even scholars will find this volume useful in introducing postmodernism and stirring the interest of students, who can then broaden their understanding of the subject through more detailed reading.[2]

In other words, I know that I am painting here in broad strokes. Consequently, the portrait of world views will necessarily lack detail. Nonetheless, I am convinced that the portrait of world views offered here is sufficiently accurate to give a newcomer a reliable guide to explore these world views in greater detail on his own and will allow him to seek out experts for further guidance.

The American James W. Sire has written extensively about the development of the concept of world views for almost forty years.[3] I will make use of some of his work in this chapter. Two of his observations about world views are important for our purposes. First, Sire notes: "two central characteristics of worldviews: their *presuppositional* character and their possible answers to the most fundamental question we can ask"[4] (emphasis in the original). In our terms, the presuppositional character of world views may be understood as the antecedents (Sire also refers to presuppositions as "commitments") upon which a world view must depend. In other words, for a world view to

[2] Dennis McCallum, ed., *The Death of Truth: What's Wrong with Multiculturalism, the Rejection of Reason, and the New Postmodern Diversity* (Minneapolis, Minn.: Bethany House, 1996), p. 9.

[3] See his *Naming the Elephant: Worldview as a Concept* (Downer's Grove, Ill.: IVP Academic, 2004), and his *The Universe Next Door*, 5th ed. (Downer's Grove, Ill.: IVP Academic, 2009).

[4] Sire, *Naming the Elephant*, p. 15.

be a true account, certain prior conditions must also be true. We may understand Sire's reference to "the most fundamental question we can ask" as having to do with both the antecedents and the consequents of a given world view. In other words, both the roots and reach of a world view must be acknowledged (we will discuss shortly why simple acknowledgment is not enough—much work must be done once a world view is identified).

We must also understand Sire's use of "presuppositional" in a second sense. *Naming the Elephant* and the sources Sire cites make clear that the antecedents of a world view (to use our vocabulary) are very often merely presupposed and not examined adequately, if at all. The presuppositional character of world views and of the composition of the Ethical Wedding Cake presents us with a challenge and an opportunity. Socrates said that the "unexamined life is not worth living." We might also say, "The unexamined world view is fraught with cognitive and moral peril." Recall the story from the first chapter about the youngsters who had equated freedom with license. Once I helped them examine the presuppositions of their position, they were very eager to get rid of it and to find a replacement.

If we merely identify our respective world views, we run the risk of falling into the traps inherent in the "values clarification" movement of the 1970s.[5] The point of values clarification exercises was not to identify an objectively correct moral evaluation of a given issue. The point was to help you to identify what it is that *you* value (or disvalue). As we will see later in this work, values clarification, left unassisted, opens the door to moral relativism, which claims that there are no right or wrong answers to moral questions. Your values are different from mine—therefore,

[5] Sidney B. Simon was a pioneer in this movement.

what might be right for you might not be right for me, and vice versa. Yes, I would like each reader to come to clarity about the nature of his own world view. I also intend to provide the reader with guidance for the evaluation and modification of his world view as well as guidance for learning how to evaluate fairly the world views of others. Learning how to evaluate world views, and learning how to correct one's own, will be a great service to us as individuals and as a community. Therefore, we may see this reflection on world views to be a great opportunity.

At the same time, the discovery of world views presents a great challenge. Let's not forget that Socrates made a pest of himself as he sought to identify and evaluate his own world view, and he got himself killed identifying and evaluating the world views of others. Likewise, inviting people to the difficult and often painful task of self-examination, evaluation, critique, and correction is not the most reliable path to popularity. Moreover, suggesting to others that their world views may be rationally incoherent or morally dubious can easily cause offense. In today's climate, such efforts might win one the labels of "close-minded", "judgmental", "intolerant", or "self-righteous".

Even at the risk of such criticisms, I must insist that one has a duty to oneself to become intellectually virtuous and morally sound, and one cannot do so if he is unaware of his presuppositions and their cognitive and ethical import. In addition, identifying and evaluating world views is indispensable if one is to evaluate the spoken and written words of others. It is difficult to converse fruitfully with someone who does not understand you or who is not understood by you. Identifying and evaluating the world view of another is the first step to having an honest and useful conversation about the most important questions one can ask of oneself and others.

Now let's get specific and offer a concrete definition of the concept of world view and identify the questions that a world view attempts to answer. After many years of scholarly research on world views, and after five editions of *The Universe Next Door: A Basic Worldview Catalog*, Sire offers the following definition of a world view: "A worldview is a commitment, a fundamental orientation of the heart, that can be expressed as a story or in a set of presuppositions (assumptions which may be true, partially true or entirely false) that we hold (consciously or subconsciously, consistently or inconsistently) about the basic constitution of reality, and that provides the foundation on which we live and move and have our being."[6]

Sire goes on for the rest of the chapter unpacking that definition. Here, I simply wish to call attention to a few significant features. First, in speaking of a world view as a "fundamental orientation of the heart", he is not at all suggesting that a world view is primarily emotional or sentimental. Borrowing from David Naugle, Sire defines the heart as "the central defining element of the human person".[7] In other words, the heart is understood as the core identity of the whole person, including both rational and *non*rational (not *ir*rational) elements.

So understood, a world view is how a person sees, understands, feels, and encounters that which, in that world view, is true and good. Paradoxically, the world view is both an expression of what the person believes is true and good, and it is also the world view's available truths and values impinging upon the person. An important step in self-knowledge is coming to clarity about one's world view. Likewise, an important step in *communication*

[6] Sire, *Universe Next Door*, p. 20.
[7] Ibid., p. 20.

with others is identifying the world views of one's conversation partners. One can have a clearer sense of what to expect—what another may understand by what one says and what may be rejected of what one says—if one knows that one is speaking with, say, someone who espouses the world view of an atheist, an agnostic, a deist, or a theist.

So far, we have looked at the import of a world view in general and at the significance of the concept of a world view for our purposes in particular. Now, following Sire's lead, let's look at the structures that are common to all world views. He identifies eight basic questions that every world view addresses.[8] I will use his list of questions, but comment on them in my own way.

1. "What is the prime reality—the really real?" This question concerns what I will call in chapter 4 "the ingredients of the real". Is prime reality physical matter? Is prime reality something that transcends physical matter? Is fundamental reality constituted by the laws of nature or by the nature of God (or of the gods)?

2. "What is the nature of external reality, that is, the world around us?" (Although Sire uses the term "external reality", I prefer the term "extramental reality".) The question concerns the reality of what might or might not exist apart from our own thoughts. Is what we call the world simply a projection of our own fantasy, or does the world have an objective reality apart from whatever we may or may not think of it?

3. "What is a human being?" The question concerns what I call philosophical anthropology, the reasoned

account of what it means to be a human person. Is a person only a very sophisticated animal? Is a person an illusion? Merely a social construct? Made in the image and likeness of God? How is a person like and unlike other kinds of existents?

4. "What happens to a person at death?" Is death final? Is a person reincarnated into another (human or non-human) life? Is human fulfillment to be found (only) after death?

5. "Why is it possible to know anything at all?" I think it is better to ask, "What can we know and why can we know it?" To Sire's question, one might answer, for example, "God implants knowledge within us" or "our consciousness evolved through a long process of evolution." My question is concerned with the *medium* of knowing (as Sire's question is) but is also concerned with the *content* of knowledge. "What is the content of our knowledge?" might variously be answered by "we can only know empirically verifiable data" or "we can know transcendent objective truths" or "we can only know our own private opinions and fantasies."

6. "How do we know what is right and wrong?" This question addresses how we come to have moral knowledge. Is knowledge of right and wrong revealed by God? By God alone? Is knowledge of right and wrong to be had simply by a knowledge of what is legal and illegal? Is knowledge of right and wrong to be had by a reflection upon the nature of the human person? Is knowledge of right and wrong simply an accumulation of what evolution has shown us to be the "best practices" for survival? Again, let's make the distinction between the *source* of moral knowledge and the *content* of moral knowledge. What actually *is*

right or wrong is a very complex issue, and I intend to show that it is the product of the interactions of a world view and the Ethical Wedding Cake.

7. "What is the meaning of human history?" Is human history going anywhere? Is there a purpose or a goal? Does history repeat itself? If so, for how long? Eternally? Can there be a fulfillment of human history? If so, is it to be found in a paradise on earth or in the hereafter? What does it mean to succeed or fail as a human individual? As a human community?

8. "What personal, life-orienting core commitments are consistent with this worldview?" For a theist, the answer might be: "To do the will of God." For a naturalist, the answer might be: "To realize my personal potential." For our purposes, the concern for consistency is very important. Intellectual and moral maturity and integrity demand that we live in a manner consistent with what we know to be true and good. Also, to avoid being a fool or a guilty bystander, one must be able to identify when the words and actions of others are consistent or inconsistent with their espoused world views. In this book, I will go a step beyond Sire and also ask, "What *communal*, life-orienting core commitments are consistent with this world view?" How shall we, in our various communities, great and small, live in a manner consistent with our world view?

In *The Universe Next Door*, Sire takes the reader on a guided tour of a wide variety of world views, stopping along the way to see how each world view answers each of the eight questions described above. For those who are interested in that level of detail about world views, Sire's book is a rewarding read. Our purposes here are somewhat different. Here, we will attend to world views as a way of understanding the reach, in terms of antecedents and consequents, of various configurations of the Ethical Wedding Cake. Attention to world views in this context will reward the thoughtful person with self-knowledge and an opportunity for honest reflection and self-criticism. It will also afford a thoughtful person a means of understanding others and why they think, choose, and act as they do.

There is another benefit to a study of world views. It affords one an opportunity to identify and evaluate very long-term trends in communities, cultures, and civilizations. In various times and places, one world view or another may be predominant. Over time, the regnant world view is likely to be overtaken by another. The transition from one dominant world view to another is not to be thought of as always clean, absolute, and without overlap. There may be significant minorities (and, surely, individuals) who espouse a world view different from the world view more commonly held.

I maintain that a study of history and culture, with an emphasis on observing the transitions from one predominant world view to another, allows one to see significant patterns. I hope to show in the remainder of the chapter that, at least in the Western world, over a time of about two thousand years, the transition between predominant world views represents what I call a progressive evacuation of the transcendent and of the personal. I do not judge this progression to be beneficial for the promotion and preservation of human good. I also maintain that a survey of world views, noting this progression, will help to make clear the urgent importance of getting right our Ethical Wedding Cake. Quoting David Naugle, Sire notes that "worldviews spring from the totality of human psychological existence intellectually in the cognition of reality, affectively in the appraisal of life, and volitionally in the active performance of the will."[9] With that in mind, I think we will see, as we trace a line through the history of predominant world views in the West, that the line leads away from human dignity and human fulfillment.

Let's start with a summary of Sire's treatment of theism from the second chapter of *The Universe Next Door*. The reader should note that Sire's treatment of theism is specifically Christian and that Christian commitment is not absolutely necessary for our purposes. Consequently, the summary of theism below is more "generic" than what one would find in Sire's actual text:

1. God is infinite and personal, transcendent and immanent, omniscient, sovereign, and good.
2. God created the cosmos *ex nihilo* to operate with a uniformity of natural causes in an open system. (The open system will be discussed in detail in the next chapter.)
3. Human beings are created in the image of God and thus possess personality, self-transcendence, intelligence, morality, gregariousness, and creativity.
4. Human beings can know both the world around them and God himself because God has built into them the capacity to do so and because he takes an active role in communicating with them.
5. For each person, death is either the gate to life with God and his people or the gate to eternal separation from the only thing that will ultimately fulfill human aspirations.
6. Ethics is transcendent and is based on the character of God as good (holy and loving).

[9] Sire, *Naming the Elephant*, p. 26.

7. History is linear, a meaningful sequence of events leading to the fulfillment of God's purposes for humanity.

It is worth noting here that in this world view, what is first and what is final is transcendent, that is, beyond the physical. Human persons have their origin and ultimate future anchored in the transcendent. This world view, as we will see later in this work, presents the human individual and the human community with grave duties, promising opportunities, and strict limits. It is also in this world view, wherein the supreme and present reality is a perfectly good God, that the problem of evil is most acute.

The world view of deism, as described in the third chapter of *The Universe Next Door*, has strong similarities to that of theism, insofar as the predominant reality is a transcendent God, but it is significantly different from that of theism in that it takes a first step away from the view of God as personal. That first step, as we shall see, is momentous.

1. A transcendent God, as a First Cause, created the universe but then left it to run on its own. God is thus not immanent, not fully personal, not sovereign over human affairs, not providential.

2. The cosmos God created is determined because it is created as a uniformity of cause and effect in a closed system: closed to God's reordering, because he is not interested in it. Closed to human reordering, because it is locked up in a clocklike fashion.

3. Human beings, though personal, are a part of the clockwork of the universe.

4. The cosmos, this world, is understood to be in its normal state; it is not fallen or abnormal. We can

know the universe, and we can determine what God is like by studying it.

5. Ethics is limited to general revelation; because the universe is normal, it reveals what is right.

6. History is linear, for the course of the cosmos was determined at creation.

The God of deism, less involved in the non-divine than the God of theism, we will see, makes fewer demands upon humanity but also offers humanity less. Because of the *im*personal character of the transcendent God, human life begins to become more oriented toward the material world. Not able to claim, as theists are and do, that they are made in the image and likeness of God, deists will find themselves at pains to account for what is distinctively human. We shall see that the loss of the personhood of God imperils the transcendence of both God and man.

In chapter 4 of *The Universe Next Door*, Sire begins his treatment of the world view of naturalism. In this world view, reality is orderly, intelligible, and finite. There is no room for (and, on this view, no need for) the transcendent or the supernatural. All of the real is available to the human mind through exclusively human efforts, and the most privileged of these efforts is the scientific method. In its later forms, naturalism holds that anything intellectually respectable can only be found in the form of the physical sciences. Sire's observations on naturalism may be summarized as follows:

1. Matter exists eternally and is all there is. God does not exist.

2. The cosmos exists as a uniformity of cause and effect in a closed system.

3. Human beings are complex "machines"; personality is an interrelation of chemical and physical properties we do not yet fully understand.
4. Death is extinction of personality and individuality.
5. History is a linear stream of events linked by cause and effect without an overarching purpose.
6. Ethics is related only to human beings.

What is particularly significant in naturalism is its mechanistic view of nature and man. Nature is a great machine that has simply emerged over time. It is infinitely malleable in the hands and minds of men. Science and human industry can overcome the limits and imperfections of nature. According to theism, it is God's grace and human ingenuity that perfect nature; according to naturalism, it is human ingenuity alone that perfects nature. A similar observation applies to man. In theism, God's grace and man's cooperation perfect man; in naturalism, humans are perfectible by human effort alone under the guidance of human wisdom and goodness. Nature may be understood, controlled, manipulated, and perfected; according to naturalism, the same may be said of human nature.

Herein lies a paradox at the heart of naturalism. On the one hand, man is simply one thing among many in the natural order. Man is a machine/animal and can be studied and understood and controlled as well as any other machine or animal. On the other hand, man is a superior being, the one who can study and understand and control. He can master himself and the rest of the real, through science, trusting human wisdom to guide him.

This confidence in the natural sciences and human ingenuity and goodness gave rise to a variety of movements, the effects of which are still very much with us today, including the move from natural to social Darwinism as well as the emergence of utilitarianism, Marxism, eugenics, and secular humanism. Absent a grand designer, naturalism can find no grand design in reality. It falls to man to make the most of himself and the world. But to what end? The difficulty in answering that question leads to the next world view to be considered here, that of nihilism.

The world view of nihilism[10] is difficult to describe. It is not something that has been worked out systematically by a dedicated school of thought. Sire observes:

> Nihilism is more a feeling than a philosophy, more a solitary stance before the universe than a worldview. Strictly speaking, nihilism is a denial of any philosophy or worldview—a denial of the possibility of knowledge, a denial that anything is valuable. If it proceeds to the absolute denial of everything, it even denies the reality of existence itself. In other words, nihilism is the negation of everything—knowledge, ethics, beauty, reality. In nihilism no statement has validity; nothing has meaning. Everything is gratuitous, *de trop*, that is, just there.[11]

Sire claims that the emptiness of nihilism is the inevitable outcome of naturalism. The impersonal character of nature, with its blind and inexorable mechanistic workings, leaves man, fundamentally, as simply a pain-collector hurtling through the darkness toward oblivion. Reality cannot know man, and all of man's efforts are futile. Bertrand Russell offers what I call the "Apostles' Creed" of nihilism:

> That Man is the product of causes which had no prevision of the end they were achieving; that his origin, his

---

[10] From the Latin word *nihil*, meaning "nothing".
[11] Sire, *Universe Next Door*, p. 94 (italics added).

growth, his hopes and fears, his loves and his beliefs, are but the outcome of accidental collocations of atoms; that no fire, no heroism, no intensity of thought and feeling, can preserve an individual life beyond the grave; that all the labours of the ages, all the devotion, all the inspiration, all the noonday brightness of human genius, are destined to extinction in the vast death of the solar system, and that the whole temple of Man's achievement must inevitably be buried beneath the débris of a universe in ruins—all these things, if not quite beyond dispute, are yet so nearly certain, that no philosophy which rejects them can hope to stand. Only within the scaffolding of these truths, only on the firm foundation of unyielding despair, can the soul's habitation henceforth be safely built.[12]

Nihilism depicts the absolute evacuation of the transcendent and the personal from the real. But to say even that is not to do justice to nihilism. Nihilism is the experience of the smothering nothingness of reality. It represents an absolute loss of meaning. For our purposes here, it is important to note, as Sire observes, that nihilism is the inevitable product of naturalism. Let's review briefly why Sire maintains this position. Doing so will provide some useful lessons as we move to our chapter on metaphysics.

Sire speaks of three "bridges" linking naturalism and nihilism. The first bridge is "Necessity and Chance". Recall that Russell spoke of man as "the product of causes which had no prevision of the end they were achieving; that his origin, his growth, his hopes and fears, his loves and his beliefs, are but the outcome of accidental collocations of

---

[12] Bertrand Russell, *Mysticism and Logic*, pp. 47–48, as cited in John Hick, *Death and Eternal Life* (Louisville, Ky.: Westminster John Knox Press, 1994), p. 150.

atoms". Human life, indeed, everything we have referred to as "real", is simply the result of unit particles of matter randomly clumping together. This universalization of chance makes all of reality an inevitable random event, a determined indeterminacy. In the closed, interlocking, mechanistic world view of naturalism, absent the "watchmaker" of deism, the coming together and interactions of unit particles of matter is random, purposeless, and inescapable. Sire states this point succinctly: "But what is chance? Either chance is the inexorable proclivity of reality to happen as it does, appearing to be chance because we do not know the reason for what happens (making chance another name for our ignorance of the forces of determinism), or it is absolutely irrational."[13]

What does this portend for human life? On this view, man is the result of the interplay of blind, irresistible forces, leading him from nowhere to nowhere:

> In a closed universe, in other words, freedom must be a *determinacy unrecognized*, and for those who work out its implications, this is not enough to allow for self-determinacy or moral responsibility.... A human being is thus a mere piece of machinery, a toy—complicated, very complicated, but a toy of impersonal cosmic forces.... The nihilists follow this argument, which can now be stated briefly: Human beings are conscious machines without the ability to affect their own destiny or do anything significant; therefore, human beings as valuable beings are dead.[14]

In other words, naturalism, rejecting even the watchmaker deity of deism, precludes the possibility of human

---

[13] Sire, *Universe Next Door*, p. 101.
[14] Ibid., p. 100 (emphasis in the original).

beings having what is necessary to live a purposeful and morally significant life. And that point brings us to the second bridge between naturalism and nihilism, which Sire calls "The Great Cloud of Unknowing".

Sire summarizes the issue neatly: "The metaphysical presupposition that the cosmos is a closed system has implications not only for metaphysics but also for epistemology. The argument in brief is this: if any given person is the result of impersonal forces—whether working haphazardly or by inexorable law—that person has no way of knowing whether what he or she seems to know is illusion or truth."[15]

One of the inevitable consequents of naturalism is that there are only facts, that is, only certain configurations of material—unit particles of matter of no interest in leading any mind to truth. One who espouses naturalism has no basis for asserting that his knowledge claims are anything other than random yet inevitable side-effects of arrangements of particles. In other words, there is no basis for claiming that the nonrational can give rise to rational knowing. Here Sire quotes C. S. Lewis to good effect:

> If all that exists is Nature, the great mindless interlocking event, if our own deepest convictions are merely the byproducts of an irrational process, then clearly there is not the slightest ground for supposing that our sense of fitness and our consequent faith in uniformity tell us anything about a reality external to ourselves. Our convictions are simply a fact *about us*—like the colour of our hair. If Naturalism is true we have no reason to trust our conviction that Nature is uniform.[16]

[15] Ibid., p. 103.
[16] C. S. Lewis, *Miracles*, p. 109, in Sire, *Universe Next Door*, p. 104 (emphasis in the original).

Nihilism acknowledges that it has arrived where natural-ism has brought it—to a state where there are no knowers and nothing known, only arrangements of matter, some of which tend to make unjustifiable claims upon the truth, as if there were such a thing as truth.

As I write this chapter, I have also been engaging in an e-mail exchange with my friend Father Joseph Fessio, S.J. He has a longstanding interest in mathematics and science. Last week, I overheard him speaking to a young Jesuit about his (Fessio's) fascination with the mathematical concept of pi. So I forwarded to him a snippet from the Internet that I had stumbled upon: "Thirty-nine decimal places of pi suffice for computing the circumference of a circle girding the known universe with an error no greater than the radius of a hydrogen atom.—Provided by Random-History.com."

Fessio quickly replied: "Thanks. I already knew this, though. Last time I checked, though, it was calculated to over 4 billion decimal places. God keeps us busy finding out things He already knows."

A theist might smile and offer a prayer of thanksgiving for being able to find traces of God's rationality and humor in nature. A deist might smile and simply marvel at being able to find traces of God's rationality in nature. A naturalist might scowl and shake his head disapprovingly at the theist and deist for anthropomorphizing nature's marvelous but impersonal orderliness. The nihilist, of course, could, at most, emit sounds that the confluence of material particles inevitably caused him to emit.

Sire describes the third bridge between naturalism and nihilism as "Is and Ought". For the naturalist, the world is simply given—it just is. Ethics is about oughtness—what ought to be and what ought not to be. How does one derive the moral "ought" from the natural "is"?

Naturalism, Sire observes, insists that one cannot derive an "ought" from an "is":

> Naturalism places us as human beings in an ethically relative box. For us to know what values within that box are true values, we need a measure imposed on us from outside the box; we need a moral plumb line by which we can evaluate the conflicting moral values we observe in ourselves and others. But there is nothing outside the box; there is no moral plumb line, no ultimate, nonchanging standard of value. Ergo: ethical nihilism.[17]

Based on what we have seen so far, we may say that the loss of the transcendent in naturalism leads to the loss of the personal—both human and divine. In the loss of the transcendent and the personal, taken together, we have the distinctive features of nihilism. Reality is inert; there is neither the knower nor the known; there can be no moral agency; there can be no purpose and no meaning. The cosmic landscape is flat, and there is nowhere to go.

Summing up the bridges that lead from naturalism to nihilism, Sire leaves us with a chilling image:

"The strands of epistemological, metaphysical and ethical nihilism weave together to make a rope long enough and strong enough to hang a whole culture. The name of the rope is Loss of Meaning. We end in a total despair of ever seeing ourselves, the world and others as in any way significant. Nothing has meaning."[18]

Here the reader may well ask, "*How* can anyone live as a nihilist? *Does* anyone live as a nihilist?" As we move through the rest of this book, I hope to show that no one can or does live as a nihilist—but I do not want the reader to toss

---

[17] Sire, *Universe Next Door*, p. 109.
[18] Ibid., p. 111.

nihilism aside as forgettable or inconsequential. As we will see in the next chapter on metaphysics, nihilism is what reality must look like if we get our metaphysics wrong.

I give the following image to my students: "Deists and naturalists can be very lovely and enjoyable people. They can make excellent dinner companions. They can be relied upon to show up with a good bottle of wine, appreciate good food, and are often witty and engaging conversationalists. But when you let the deists into your home, the naturalists come in right behind them, and the naturalists always unwittingly leave the back door open for the nihilists, who inevitably arrive and spoil the dinner for everyone—before killing all the guests and hosts and then burning down the house."

There are many who find nihilism to be unbearable or unnecessary but who do not want to accept the transcendence insisted upon by theism and deism. These people try to carve out a safe space apart from the mechanism of naturalism, the barrenness of nihilism, and the loftiness of theism and deism. Thus it remains for us to consider two more world views—existentialism and postmodernism.

Let's pause for a moment and reflect on the optimism of naturalism and the bleakness of nihilism. Naturalism is characterized by a serene confidence in the power of reason (here understood as the work of the physical sciences) and the highest hopes for the perfection of man and society by his own efforts. In contrast, nihilism, which Sire sees as the inevitable offspring and heir of naturalism, is sterile and dark. Nietzsche, the godfather of nihilism, if you will, lamented that people could not or would not see and embrace the truth and consequents of nihilism. Nietzsche saw that the transition from theism to deism to naturalism to nihilism represented steps toward the slow and inevitable death of God. He was embittered that few would join him in celebrating the demise of the divine. In his disturbing "Parable of the Madman", Nietzsche sees to his dismay that people are not yet ready to admit the emergence of nihilism that man himself has brought about:

> The madman jumped into their midst and pierced them with his eyes. "Whither is God?" he cried; "I will tell you. *We have killed him*—you and I. All of us are his murderers.... How shall we comfort ourselves, the murderers of all murderers? What was holiest and mightiest of all that the world has yet owned has bled to death under our knives: who will wipe this blood off us? What water is there for us to clean ourselves? What festivals of atonement, what sacred games shall we have to invent? Is not the greatness of this deed too great for us? Must we ourselves not become gods simply to appear worthy of it? There has never been a greater deed; and whoever is born after us—for the sake of this deed he will belong to a higher history than all history hitherto."
>
> Here the madman fell silent and looked again at his listeners; and they, too, were silent and stared at him in astonishment. At last he threw his lantern on the ground, and it broke into pieces and went out. "I have come too early," he said then; "my time is not yet. This tremendous event is still on its way, still wandering; it has not yet reached the ears of men. Lightning and thunder require time; the light of the stars requires time; deeds, though done, still require time to be seen and heard. This deed is still more distant from them than most distant stars—*and yet they have done it themselves.*[19]

Nihilism's time had not yet come. The world view of naturalism did not yet have a crisis of faith, that is to say,

[19] Friedrich Nietzsche, *The Gay Science*, trans. Walter Kaufmann (New York: Vintage, 1974), pp. 181–82 (emphasis in original).

a crisis of its faith in the wisdom of scientific (empirical/mechanistic) reason and its faith in the fundamental goodness and perfectibility of man by his own efforts. Fueled by the might of industrialization and guided by a confident and progressively bureaucratic utilitarianism, the human future looked bright indeed. There was no reason to doubt the path that man was on. But a crisis of faith in reason and man did come—in the form of the First World War.

The First World War, at the outset, was heralded as a "glorious little war", and nations were promised that "Our boys will be home by Christmas." It was not to be.

The First World War was the first mechanized war fought on a grand scale. The old and the new clashed, with tragic results. Cavalry charges and bayonet charges met with tanks, machines guns, and poison gas. Europe had never seen such rapid slaughter. At the First Battle of the Marne, at the outset of the war, there were over 500,000 killed and wounded in a week's fighting.

After the war, more than just cities and empires lay in ruins. Naturalism's faith in the inevitable success and progress of reason and man proved to be unwarranted. One could easily imagine Nietzsche's madman lighting his lantern again, expecting a better hearing this time as he made his rounds announcing the death of God. Even so, nihilism is a bitter pill to swallow. Naturalism was in tatters, but culture at large could not quite bring itself to welcome Nietzsche's madman and embrace nihilism.

After the Second World War, with even greater slaughter, the need to replace naturalism was more urgent. The aftermath of the Holocaust and the use of nuclear weapons and the emergence of the Iron Curtain and the Cold War, taken together, precluded the high hopes that had marked the outset of the twentieth century. There must be a worthy response to the absurdity and horror of the first half of the twentieth century. Theism and deism had long since been discarded as discredited. Naturalism was an embarrassment. Nihilism offered no satisfaction. From the ashes there emerged existentialism.

Existentialism is a complex phenomenon; there is no simple, common understanding of what it is or what it means or of who is or is not an existentialist. Fortunately, it is not our task to offer a definitive account of existentialism. In this context, it is sufficient to work out an account of existentialism that shows that it is, among other things, a response to the unpalatable and unlivable nature of the world view of nihilism. We attend to this world view because it is one that has had great influence on life, thought, and art in the West for much of the twentieth century. We also need to understand existentialism so that we can identify and evaluate its corresponding Ethical Wedding Cake, which many have espoused.

Nihilism is an immersion in the irresistibly bleak, barren, and absurd. Existentialism is a choice to shake one's fist defiantly against the absurdity. Perhaps an illustration will help.

When I was in high school, I had a blacklight poster in my bedroom. In the lower right-hand corner of the poster, there was a dictionary entry for the word "defiance", including three definitions. The first definition spoke of "open disobedience". The second definition, which I liked even more than the first, was "contempt of opposition". The third definition was my favorite: "disposition to resist". What could be more appealing to an adolescent male? Above the dictionary entry was an illustration depicting the essence of the definitions.

The background of the illustration was dark and gloomy. In the foreground was a little mouse. Above, a hideous bird of prey, with enormous and menacing talons, was shown swooping down on the mouse. It was clear, given their respective sizes, that the mouse was doomed. The only light in the illustration was a glow surrounding the—ahem—"significant gesture" that the mouse had extended above his head in the direction of the bird of prey. That, I believe, summarizes the stance of existentialism to reality.

Now let's flesh out that illustration with a few technical details. The import of the word "existentialism" must be understood in terms of the distinction between "existence" and "essence". The Latin root of "existence" is *existere*, which means "to stand out". "To stand out" from what? To stand out from, to stand apart from, nothingness. Existence, in other words, indicates that you are. In contrast, "essence" refers to what you are—that is to say, what kind of thing you are. Existence addresses the bare fact that you are. Essence addresses your "whatness", your nature.

The hallmark of existentialism is that "existence precedes essence." In other words, *that* you are precedes *what* you are. Granted, this may seem strange at first, but the insight is worth considering. A significant claim of existentialism is that we are the results of all of our choices. Most people, it is said, do not clearly and consciously choose. They drift through life as thoughtless followers, as sheep, going along to get along, doing whatever is expected of them, without knowing why and without really choosing to do so. Such people, as existentialism sees them, are "inauthentic" and "in bad faith".

To be authentic, existentialism maintains, one must choose one's values, consciously and deliberately. What matters most about the values chosen is not that any individual or group may approve, for their approval is irrelevant. What matters most is not that the values chosen are in harmony with human nature, for there is no such thing—existence *precedes* essence. What matters most is that *you* chose them. In the face of the unrelenting absurdity of life, you decided to stand up on your own and decided for yourself what your values are. The hero is not one who does what is expected of him; the hero is the one who does what he chooses, because he chooses to do it. In this standing up defiantly against the absurdity and the arid meaninglessness of reality, one can find meaning and even dignity.

With this rough sketch in place, let's look at a summary of Sire's account of the world view of existentialism from the sixth chapter of *The Universe Next Door*.

1. The cosmos is composed solely of matter, but to human beings reality appears in two forms—subjective and objective.
2. For human beings alone, existence precedes essence; people make themselves who they are.
3. Each person is totally free as regards his nature and destiny.
4. The highly wrought and tightly organized objective world stands over against human beings and appears absurd.
5. In full recognition of and against the absurdity of the objective world, the authentic person must revolt and create value.

Existentialism, at least in part, was an attempt to assert meaning while standing on the grave of an optimistic and fatally naïve naturalism. While offering more than nihilism, existentialism's anger and its defiance offered little solace. It placed itself between the corpse of naturalism and the abyss of nihilism. But how appealing could the futile gesture of existentialism be? With that question in mind, let's turn to the world view of postmodernism.

Of what is *post*modernism "post"? Well, modernism, of course. In Sire's terms, modernism may be another name for naturalism. Postmodernism is a rejection of naturalism/modernism's apparently boundless confidence in human reason, human goodness, and humanity's attempt to master nature. At the same time, postmodernism, like existentialism, is a shying away from the nihilism that Sire and I maintain is the inevitable result of taking naturalism to its logical conclusion. Whereas existentialism is a choice to shake one's fist angrily in defiance against the absurdity of it all, postmodernism is a choice to remain detached and whimsical, with a sense of irony and parody in the face of absurdity.

To set the stage for postmodernism, let's start with a snapshot of the smoldering ruins that resulted from the long dominance of naturalism/modernity:

> In February 1943, standing before thousands of loyal Nazis in the *Sportpalast* in Berlin, Josef Goebbels called for 'total war.' Total war it was, and with a few years the *Sportpalast* was part of the smoldering ruins of the National Socialist movement.
>
> Martin Heidegger, one of the movement's most famous former members, had said that the 'inner truth and greatness' of the Nazis' vision 'consisted in modern man's encounter with global technology.' Surveying the wreckage of the encounter after the war, the German Catholic writer Romano Guardini saw instead the completion and the collapse of the modern project. The aspirations that had inspired the founders of modern thought—the conquest of nature through science and the emancipation of power from moral restraint—had been achieved beyond anyone's wildest dreams, and they had turned to ashes before that success could be enjoyed.[20]

[20] Rein Staal, "The Forgotten Story of Postmodernity", *First Things*, December 2008, p. 35.

Traumatized by the consequences of the naturalist/ modernist exaltation of reason, objectivity, and certainty, postmodernism lurched sharply in the opposite direction. According to postmodernism, confidence in *anything*, but especially in reason, is misplaced. On this view, there is no "truth-with-a-capital-T" to be discovered. "Truth" is made. "Truth" is a social construct, a tacit or even explicit agreement that certain values will be exalted as "true" or "good" or "objective" or "obvious" or "self-evident"; these values, selected by a group that will be benefited by the exaltation of these values, are not *really* "true" or "good", etc. They are made to be accepted as "true" or "good" by the manipulation of language by the group in power.

For example, European culture is not superior to any other culture, but powerful Europeans said that their culture was superior, and less powerful people believed them, or were at least forced to appear to believe them. Men are not superior to women, but powerful men said that they were superior to women, and less powerful women believed them, etc. Here we see the fundamental insight of postmodernism—there is no such thing as "reality" as such; what we call "real" (or "good" or "true", etc.) is a function of the language of the group in power. Reality is made by the powerful, not discovered by the wise. The role of postmodernism is to identify and "deconstruct" the constructions of various dominant groups and, with irony and whimsy and parody, expose these truth claims for the shams that they are. Perhaps a few illustrations will help to make this point more clear.

Years ago, I worked at a university whose campus ministry office produced a bulletin to be distributed to the students as they left the chapel after Mass. The bulletin contained the usual information about the schedule of Masses and Confession during the week, the latest fundraising effort for this or that good cause, etc. And at the back of the bulletin was a weekly editorial entitled "Time to Make Some Meaning!" I cringed whenever I saw that title. It was so thoroughly postmodern. On this view, meaning is not found by a wise and observant knower. Meaning is "made" or "constructed" through the use of language. In other words, one takes otherwise meaningless events or phenomena and "makes" meaning of them by declaring them to be meaningful.

Seeing that editorial every week for years reminded me of a poster that I had been sent by a recruiter of a university department of modern languages when I was a high school senior. At that time, I had thought seriously about learning some modern languages and then working as a translator; I thought that such a path would provide many opportunities for travel and adventure. The poster declared: "The Limits of My Language Are the Limits of My World." At the age of seventeen, I liked the quote on the poster very much. I thought that it validated my inclination to study languages and travel. If the only language I spoke/wrote/read/understood were English, for example, very many other doors would be closed to me.

Years later, after having read a good deal of philosophy, I saw that poster could lend itself to a dangerous interpretation. First, it could be read in a way that suggested that reality is co-terminus with my language, i.e., that reality extends only as far as my language does.[21] More significantly, it could be read in a way that suggested that there really is nothing true or good, that there is only what my (or my group's) language names as true or good.

---

[21] See, for example, "linguistic determinism" and Ludwig Wittgenstein's assertion that "the limits of my language mean the limits of my world" (*Tractatus Logico-Philosophicus*, proposition 5.6 [Mineola, N.Y.: Dover, 1998]).

This latter approach, as we shall see later in this book, is important both for a theory of knowledge (epistemology) and for moral methodology. Epistemologically, the claim that there really is nothing true or good, that there is only what my (or my group's) language names as true or good, is the foundation of a theory of knowledge known as "nominalism" (from the Latin *nomen*, which means "name"). According to that theory, there are no classes of things; there are no universal natures. In other words, there is nothing of a class that is good; there are only things that we *name* "good". There is no universal human nature; there are only certain things that we *name* human.

Nominalism, as a theory of knowledge, undergirds various moral methodologies known as "moral relativism". According to moral relativism, there is no universal, no objective good or evil or true or false. "What is true for you may not be true for me; what is evil in your eyes may be good in mine." Moral relativism takes the cliché "Beauty is in the eye of the beholder" and changes it to "Good (or 'evil' or 'true' or 'false') is in the eye of the beholder."

Postmodernism goes one step farther and says that "good (or 'evil' or 'true' or 'false') is in the language of the speaker (especially the speakers of the dominant group)." According to postmodernism, reality is constituted, constructed, by language. No one discovers objective reality; one simply plays the language games of different groups. If you change the language, you change the reality. Taking this to an extreme, some postmoderns claim that *all* reality is *merely* constructed by language. The role of the sophisticated thinker is to expose and to mock any and all pretense to "objectivity" or "fact" or "nature". But is such a view livable?

Alan Sokal decided to put postmodernism to the test. He published "Transgressing the Boundaries: Toward a Transformative Hermeneutics of Quantum Gravity" in the Spring/Summer 1996 issue of the journal *Social Text*. In that article, Sokal proposed that gravity is a social and linguistic construct. Think about that for a moment. Sokal proposed that gravity, a reality that affects us at every moment of our existence, often in frustrating and sometimes in very violent ways, is simply a function of language, i.e., merely a social construct.

On the date that his article was published in *Social Text*, Sokal revealed in the journal *Lingua Franca* that the article was spurious, describing it as "a pastiche of Left-wing cant, fawning references, grandiose quotations, and outright nonsense", "structured around the silliest quotations [by postmodernist academics] I could find about mathematics and physics".[22]

The editors of *Social Text* and the advocates of the postmodern thought that the journal represents were quite upset by Sokal's charade. Yes, all of reality is socially constructed and merely a function of language, but deceiving the editors of a postmodern journal is *really* wrong.

Let's stop for a moment and assess where we are now in terms of the project of this book. My purpose is to provide the reader with the means of identifying the world view, metaphysics, anthropology, and ethics embedded in any moral claim he may encounter. Once he is aware of these, he may evaluate, critique, clarify, reject, or improve upon what he has found. So able, he can begin to interpret the ambient culture in which he finds himself; he can understand better the books he reads; he can converse more astutely with those who agree or disagree with him.

---

[22] Alan Sokal, "A Physicist Experiments with Cultural Studies", *Lingua Franca*, May 1996; Alan Sokal, "What the *Social Text* Affair Does and Does Not Prove", in *A House Built on Sand: Exposing Postmodernist Myths about Science*, ed. Noretta Koertge (Oxford: Oxford University Press, 1998), p. 11.

As we move into the heart of this book, which is the exposition and analysis of the Ethical Wedding Cake, I wish to make sure that the reader understands that when one endorses, explicitly or implicitly, an Ethical Wedding Cake, the roots and import of the endorsement spread out to constitute a world view. In various times and places, a particular world view may be so widely espoused that it is not even noted, much less questioned. Such an approach to a dominant world view, an approach that is both blind and incurious, can lead to disaster for individuals, for communities, and even for civilizations. If the reader wishes to reflect on this matter further, I suggest that he turn to Glenn Tinder's *Against Fate: An Essay on Personal Dignity* and Romano Guardini's *The End of the Modern World*, as well as Sire's two books on world views that we have drawn upon in this chapter.

For now, the reader will be well served, if, having read this far, he approaches the forthcoming exposition of the Ethical Wedding Cake with this question constantly in mind: "To what kind of world view will this lead?"

CHAPTER 4

METAPHYSICS: A SYSTEMATIC ACCOUNT OF THE REAL

Philosophy's main concern is not with what the others maintain, and not even with what they presuppose. Its object is with what is irreducibly real.

—Paul Weiss, *Modes of Being*

I imagine that many readers might find the fact that this chapter is entitled "Metaphysics" to be somewhat off-putting. For those who have read little or no philosophy, "metaphysics" can sound ethereal, unreal, or simply out of touch with ordinary life. For those who have wandered around in popular bookstores, "metaphysics" suggests tarot cards, spells, and runes. For those who have read *some* philosophy, the word "metaphysics" may conjure up memories of unintelligible texts discussed in mind-numbingly boring undergraduate lecture halls. For those who have read a good deal of philosophy, especially philosophy of a certain type, the word "metaphysics" might prompt snickers and eye-rolling.

For those schooled in modern philosophy (ranging from, roughly, the sixteenth century to the early twentieth century), the term "metaphysics", at best, stood for "all unfounded and unfoundable philosophical speculation" (a memorable turn of phrase from Mortimer Adler, when speaking of Immanuel Kant). At worst, metaphysics was simply nonsense: "... if a man should talk to me of ... *immaterial substances*, or of a *free subject* ... I should not say he were in an error but that his words were without meaning—that is to say, absurd."[1] One might well ask Hobbes if he was speaking these words of his own free will, that is, as a "free subject". More importantly, Hobbes was dismissive of metaphysics because of the *meta-* in metaphysics. From the Greek, *meta-physis* literally means "beyond the physical". Hobbes, an embodiment of the naturalist world view, insisted that *only* the physical was real. We will see in this chapter why such a view, which I call "materialist reductionism", cannot be maintained.

Metaphysics, as an attempt to offer a systematic and coherent account for the real as such, is, in our postmodern era, an embarrassing and laughable attempt to do what is impossible. There can be no account of the real, because nothing is *really* real—there are only linguistic contrivances and social constructions at the service of dominant groups. Yet I maintain that metaphysics is an indispensable discipline, seeking, as Paul Weiss observed, a concern with "what is irreducibly real". What does he mean by "irreducibly"? Perhaps an example will help.

When I was an undergraduate, there was a little rhyme that was popular among physics students. They said, "Humanity is really biology; biology is really chemistry; chemistry is really physics." On their view, human reality can be reduced to its most basic components, namely, the irreducibly real physical absolute-units studied by physics. Weiss would say that the physics students stopped short. They stopped short of where philosophy should put its

---

[1] Thomas Hobbes, *Leviathan* (Indianapolis, Ind.: Hackett, 1994), pt. 1, chap. 5 (emphasis in the original).

focus, which is on the irreducible, *metaphysical* elements of the real. We will see shortly how that is done. Weiss would insist that philosophy, specifically metaphysics, identifies and explores the foundational grounding of reality. Apart from the grounding, we will have our "feet planted firmly in mid-air", to borrow a phrase from Beckwith and Koukl.[2]

We avoid the challenging work of metaphysics at our peril. Consider this: "A small error at the outset can lead to great errors in the final conclusions as the Philosopher [Aristotle] says."[3] As we saw in chapter 1, in the exposition of the Ethical Wedding Cake, the "outset", to use Aquinas' term, the foundation of the real, is accounted for by metaphysics. It is metaphysics that opens and closes doors for anthropology and ethics—in other words, it determines what is possible and impossible for them. Without a sure foundation of metaphysics on which to build, our anthropology and ethics will be just castles in the sky. Our ability to do justice to human dignity and to live as we ought in order to realize fully our human nature depends on our clarity and our accuracy regarding the metaphysical foundations. Paul Weiss wrote, "To think truly is to think freely."[4] We cannot be free apart from the truth, and we will be hobbled in our ability to stand on the truth if we do not properly identify and build upon a firm foundation of metaphysics.

Dennis McCallum, editor of the anthology *The Death of Truth*, tells a charming story that illustrates why metaphysics is an unavoidable enterprise.

---

[2] Francis Beckwith and Gregory Koukl, *Relativism: Feet Planted Firmly in Mid-Air* (Grand Rapids, Mich.: Baker Books, 1998).

[3] Saint Thomas Aquinas, *On Being and Essence*, trans. Armand Maurer (Toronto, Ontario: Pontifical Institute of Mediaeval Studies, 1987), prologue.

[4] Paul Weiss, *Nature and Man* (New York: Henry Holt, 1947), p. xii.

When ... author Ravi [Zacharias] visited Columbus to speak at The Ohio State University, his hosts took him to visit the Wexner Center for the Arts. The Wexner Center is a citadel of postmodern architecture. It has stairways leading nowhere, columns that come down but never touch the floor, beams and galleries going everywhere, and a crazy-looking exposed girder system over most of the outside. Like most of postmodernism, it defies every canon of common sense and every law of rationality. [Zacharias] looked at the building and cocked his head. With a grin he asked, "I wonder if they used the same techniques when they laid the foundation?"[5]

Postmodernism in particular is skittish about *any* references to foundations. Yet, we shall see time and again throughout this work thinkers and schools of thought making use of what they deny and being parasitic upon what they reject. In other words, they will be shown to be standing upon foundations even as they denounce or deny foundations. Zacharias knew, as the postmoderns had overlooked, that even a structure built as a tribute to postmodernism's rejection of tradition, the reliability of reason and science, and the knowledge of absolutes made use of standard engineering practices and the laws of physics—all of which would have been acknowledged by the rationalists of modernity—when putting in the foundation of that building. As a philosopher, I wish to identify the foundation, that is, the ingredients and structures of the real that enable engineers to use physics and concrete to make foundations that hold up buildings, even buildings that celebrate postmodernism.

[5] Dennis McCallum, ed., *The Death of Truth: What's Wrong with Multiculturalism, the Rejection of Reason, and the New Postmodern Diversity* (Minneapolis, Minn.: Bethany House, 1996), p. 262.

I describe metaphysics here as an attempt at a systematic and comprehensive account of what is first and final, what is primordially and ultimately real, an explanation of what is and why the real is as it is. Of course, such a project could never presume to be complete or immune to criticism, but we can at least make an effort that is worthy of a refutation. My intention here is to sketch an account of the real, including the elements of the real that may not rightly be overlooked, dismissed, or denied.[6]

In undertaking such a venture as described above, I will divide metaphysics into the constitutive and the temporal. By "constitutive" I mean the account of that dimension of the real as understood in terms of reality's most basic elements. In other words, the constitutive dimension of metaphysics addresses the question, "What are the ingredients of the real?" Most broadly construed, the constitutive dimension of metaphysics may be understood as either materialist or the properly transcendent. These options are mutually exclusive. I will consider the materialist option first.

The materialist option may most aptly be thought of as reminiscent of ancient Greek atomism, which asserts that the real is composed only of atoms in the void (that is, unit particles in empty space). We can substitute for "atoms" all the elementary particles that physical science has discovered since the twentieth century. I prefer the term "absolute-units", so that we might include particles, waves, and fields. So understood, the fundamental thesis of materialism is that nothing exists that is not an absolute-unit or a composition of absolute-units.

Put more simply, a materialist will claim to have drawn up an exhaustive list of the ingredients of the real. That list

[6] See the chart at the end of this chapter for a schematic of metaphysics.

would read as follows: (1) absolute-units; (2) empty space. That's it. If it cannot be made up of what is referred to on that list, then it cannot be real. To get some practice in Thinking in Four Directions, let's first look at the consequents of materialism.

Such a metaphysics could only allow for an anthropology that I call "physical reductionism". In such an anthropology, the human person, *apparently* complex, is in fact "reducible" to his physical components. Man = animal; anthropology = biology. On this view, the human person is an aggregate of absolute-units that have come together to form this body. (A human person cannot have an immortal soul if that which is not physical is not real.) He is nothing more than a body.

Such an anthropology could allow for only an ethics of hedonism (from the Greek *hedone*, meaning "pleasure"). Hedonism may be summarized simply as "pleasure = good" and "pain = evil". In this context, human community *at best* would consist of hedonists who, motivated by enlightened self-interest and the fear of hangovers and the like, agree to be opportunistic but more or less polite thrill-seekers, ready to exploit others for pleasure. Here I must ask: "Is this a moral house in which we would want to live?"

I hope that this brief look at the consequents of metaphysical materialism will make clear the urgent importance of having clarity regarding the foundations upon which we build.

Now let's look at the *antecedents* of metaphysical materialism. I hope to show that metaphysical materialism cannot be true because its antecedents are incoherent. In other words, metaphysical materialism cannot be true because reality *must* be greater than the physical alone. In fact, physical reality itself *requires* the truly *meta*-physical.

As a metaphysical account, the constitutive as materialist, and its consequent anthropology and ethics, as described above, is untenable. Ironically, materialism, which maintains that only the physical is real, cannot account for physical bodies. That is a rather embarrassing failure for materialism.

Remember that materialism offers a "two-ingredient" account of the real. *Everything* is accounted for by what is on the exhaustive list of the ingredients of the real: (1) absolute-units; (2) empty space. Whatever cannot be accounted for by what is on the *exhaustive* list cannot be real. All right—let's put materialism to the test.

When I teach this segment in class, I draw the exhaustive list of the ingredients of the real on the board. Then I hold up a pen before the students and ask, "What is this?" They answer, "It's a pen." I ask them, "Is the pen empty space?" They answer, "No." Then I draw a line through "empty space" on the board. I ask, "Is the pen an absolute-unit? In other words, is everything that is real made up of pens?" "No", they answer. Then I draw a line through "absolute-unit" on the board. I ask, "Is the pen real?" In chorus they reply, "Yes." Then, while pointing to the crossed-out exhaustive list of the ingredients of the real, I ask the question that, I know through years of teaching, inevitably causes an awkward silence: "Does anyone see a problem?"

I know from experience that some of them do see the problem but cannot quite articulate it. So, I help them out: "On the one hand, you say that the pen is real. On the other hand, you say that on materialism's exhaustive list of the ingredients of the real we find only 'absolute-units' and 'empty space'. So ... how can the pen be real? Or, if the pen is real, how can the list be exhaustive? Either the pen is not real, or the list is not exhaustive, not complete."

The students rightly observe that no one ever claimed that the pen is an absolute-unit. "It is a body", they say. Yes, and what is a body? "A body is absolute-units together." And what is a "together"? Silence. Is it empty space? "No." Is it an absolute-unit? "No." Well then, according to materialism, either "together" is an absolute-unit, or it is empty space, or it is not real. And, students, if "together" is not real, then your account of the pen as a body that is "absolute-units together" cannot be correct, which puts the reality of the pen in doubt.

Each semester, when I teach this segment, the same alternatives to "together" are trotted out: The absolute-units are not *together*; they are *joined* or *composed* or *proximate* or *interactive*. The change of name does not change the reality. For bodies to be real, there must be some non-physical reality, in this case, a *relation* that exists among the absolute-units of which the body is composed. The advocates of materialism have severely handicapped themselves. They must account for bodies, which are a familiar part of our ordinary experience. By their own admission, they only have absolute-units (which by definition are irreducible) and empty space to work with. They will admit that the world is not made up of pens like the one I hold before my students; pens *are* reducible. Therefore, they must account for the physical body of the pen that they admit is real, but they cannot account for it, because their list of the ingredients of the real does not allow them to. The pen is not empty space; the pen is not an absolute-unit. There must be a third category of reality, a non-physical-something-else (in this case, a relation) in addition to absolute-units and empty space.

In the past, I have found that students have a hard time accepting this segment of the course; I think that they over-complicate the issue. So, I will try to restate the issue as clearly as I am able: The absolute-units that form the pen—are they together? If not, then there is no pen, only separate absolute-units. But that is incoherent. There is a pen, and the world is not constituted by pens but by absolute-units in composition, that is to say, in a *relation* that is not material.

The position I am taking, while admittedly far-reaching (as I will show throughout this book), is actually quite modest. I am maintaining that the real is not limited to the physical. If this position is not true, then we will be at pains to explain the existence of bodies—a rather embarrassing position for a materialist to be in.

Now we are in a position to start to see links between what we are discussing here and the topics we have covered in previous chapters. Let's recall the chapter on world views and think back to our criticism of naturalism. Following Sire, we saw that naturalism inevitably leads to a slide toward nihilism. We also see that disaffected naturalists who cannot stomach nihilism can turn to existentialism or postmodernism—but these latter world views have problems of their own. Thus we can see that naturalism can be criticized in terms of its consequents, namely, the horror of nihilism and the distractions of existentialism and postmodernism. Having examined metaphysics in terms of constitutive materialism, we can now look at naturalism afresh, this time looking at it in terms of its *antecedents*.

For the world view of naturalism to be true, what else must be true? In other words, what are the prior truths that would allow naturalism to be true? The mechanistic view of nature advocated by those who espouse naturalism demands that a metaphysics of constitutive materialism be true. But we have just seen that materialism is in fact incoherent, as it cannot account for physical bodies. This fact is not only an embarrassment for materialism. This fact is also a sharp blow to naturalism. Naturalism, as we saw in the last chapter, is untenable in terms of its consequents; now we can see that it is also untenable in terms of its antecedents. We will see later, in chapters 5 and 6, respectively, that naturalism and materialism lead to an incoherent anthropology and an unlivable ethics.

Very often, I tell my students, "If you pull on a thread, you get the whole rug." In other words, reality is a complete package. When one makes a moral claim, one *always* brings along with it a moral methodology, an anthropology, a metaphysics, and a world view. A world view always brings with it a corresponding Ethical Wedding Cake, whether one knows it or not, whether one likes it or not. You cannot cobble together an account of the real from parts that do not fit together. Only a true account of the real is coherent and livable. A poor choice in world view, metaphysics, or anthropology *always* leads to an incoherent account of the real and an unlivable ethics. That is why developing the habit of Thinking in Four Directions is so important. A lot of ink and blood are unnecessarily spilled when individuals, communities, or civilizations do not have the habit of Thinking in Four Directions.

*

Clearly, constitutive materialism must be rejected. Consequently, we turn toward the constitutive transcendental. This view of metaphysics allows for what materialism does not, namely, the existence of the nonmaterial. Such a view of metaphysics can ground an anthropology and ethics that are up to the task of accounting for human dignity and relations, and a metaphysics that is open to the possibility of encountering what is suprahuman. To understand the import of these claims more fully, we now turn our attention to the dimension of metaphysics that I refer to as the temporal.

My goal in this section of the present chapter is to show the importance of learning how to inhabit "time lucidly and unreservedly".[7] My understanding of the importance of time has been greatly influenced by the philosopher Glenn Tinder. I have been reading and rereading his book *Against Fate* for over twenty-five years. In that book, he outlines the urgency of understanding well how human life, lived both as individuals and as a community, must be accounted for in terms of its relation to what is inside and outside of time. Humans, alone and together, lose themselves without a knowing integration of past, present, and future:

> We are told, of course, that the moment is all that we can ever have and that we should therefore live for it. This is a message implicit in much entertainment and advertising and it is given philosophical form in the doctrine of hedonism. But trying to grasp being and selfhood in the present, while ignoring the past and the future is like trying to grasp a handful of water; it is gone the instant one takes hold. We not only *have* a past and future, we *are* our past and future. To be confined to the present moment, therefore, is to be alienated from oneself and in that sense to be nothing. The only genuine and realizable present is one in which the past and future are focused and harmonized. It is a space in which the past and the future, rather than being excluded, as when the present is conceived of as a chronological segment of time, meet in the temporal experience of a receptive human being. A real present presupposes continuity. The fragmentation of

[7] Glenn Tinder, *Against Fate: An Essay on Personal Dignity* (Notre Dame, Ind.: University of Notre Dame Press, 1981), p. 147.

time, alienating us from the past and future, alienates us from the real present as well.[8]

Our current ambient culture, emphasizing the transitory and the immediate through the constant flickering of stimuli, fosters not only *attention* deficit but also *comprehension* deficit. I use "comprehension" in two senses. The first is the more familiar sense of comprehension as *understanding*. Our present manic culture impedes (I am tempted to say "precludes") our understanding of human nature and human life. More importantly, what I mean when I say that we suffer a comprehension deficit can be made clear by looking at the etymology of the word "comprehension". The roots of the word are found in the Latin *prehendere*, meaning "to grasp". What I have in mind will be made more clear if we consider the word "prehensile", from *prehensus*, which is the past participle of *prehendere*.

We know of monkeys that have "prehensile tails". These monkeys have long, flexible tails that grasp a tree branch by wrapping themselves fully around the circumference of the branch. With that image in mind, let's return to the issue of comprehension. To comprehend something in the two senses that I mean is to understand it by fully, "surroundingly" grasping the whole of something. This kind of understanding is precisely what is so difficult to achieve in our culture because our culture douses us in a constant spray of transitory and unrelated fragments. There is no whole to hold onto. We can become so dazzled by what immediately passes before us that we become unaware of the reality of the import of the past and the future impinging upon us. Consequently, we can have no grasp, no *comprehension* of who we are, as human individuals and

---

[8] Ibid., p. 129 (emphases in the original).

communities, as we are cut off from time as a whole, that is, the experience of present time as a lived bridge between past and future. Without a clear sense of our "from-which" (past) and toward-which (future), we cannot know who we are; we cannot, as Tinder said, "inhabit time lucidly and unreservedly".

Tinder writes as a political philosopher, and in his book *Against Fate*, he interprets all of history and political life in terms of our episodes of clarity and obscurity regarding time. I am writing as a philosopher and, more specifically, as a metaphysician. I am following Tinder's example, but also reaching beyond him, as I am interpreting *all of reality*, but especially all of human reality, in terms of identifying a right understanding of time. Both Tinder's project and mine require painting in broad strokes, while admitting with humility and stubbornness that we cannot and need not write an infinitely large and detailed work to deal with our infinitely large topics. Many may view such an approach with suspicion or skepticism; academic professionals may cavil at the details and particulars that are not specifically addressed. Nonetheless, *someone* must take up the challenge of offering an account of the whole. Otherwise, human knowledge and human living will suffer a limitation of vision—one might even say a blindness—that they can ill afford.

Regarding this treatment of time in relation to the whole (of both humanity and reality), I take Tinder's cautionary note about his work as a cautionary note about my own work:

Readers must be warned that so broad a goal means neglecting details, even rather large and important details sometimes, in order to try to see and identify the configurations of the whole. I try relentlessly, even if not always successfully, to look at things comprehensively.... This may sound intolerably presumptuous. One excuse I would offer is that we have little choice. We are forced to understand our situation as a whole because we are forced to live in that situation as a whole.... Specialization is the luxurious duty of scholars but is not permitted to us as (in Kierkegaard's phrase) 'existing individuals.' The folly of attempting to take in everything at a glance is properly eschewed by scholars in their capacity as scholars. If eschewed by all of us, however, it would indicate that we had forgotten that we are concrete human beings with the task of living life as a whole. If both the scholarly folly and human necessity of the tasks are kept in mind, perhaps it can be undertaken without arrogance.[9]

I hope to show that I am guilty of neither arrogance nor recklessness as I undertake this project of offering a concise (even "terse") account of the role of the temporal in metaphysics.

By temporal I mean that dimension of metaphysics which attends to the real in terms of its relation to what is within time and what is beyond time (the "supratemporal", if you will). Looking at this sentence as I have just typed it, I see that I have communicated nothing. I am reminded of conversations I had with my mother after she had suffered a stroke. One of the consequences of that brain injury is aphasia, the loss of the ability to articulate. As she sometimes struggled to express herself while I simultaneously struggled to understand her, she would shout in exasperation: "You know what I mean!"

I find myself in similar circumstances when talking about time. Everyone lives with it, in it, through it. Everyone knows what it is—but who can offer a satisfactory

---

[9] Ibid., pp. 2–3.

definition of time? I had considered speaking of time as a "sequenced duration". A quick look at the definition of duration at dictionary.com reveals: "Continuance or persistence in time" and "the length of time that something lasts or continues". Oops! A circular definition—trying to define something in terms of the thing to be defined.

I console myself in my struggles to define time by putting myself in the very good company of Saint Augustine:

> What is time? Who can explain this easily and briefly? Who can comprehend this even in thought so as to articulate the answer in words? Yet what do we speak of, in our familiar everyday conversation, more than of time? We surely know what we mean when we speak of it. We also know what is meant when we hear someone else talking about it. What then is time? Provided that no one asks me, I know. If I want to explain it to an inquirer, I do not know. But I confidently affirm myself to know that if nothing passes away, there is no past time, and if nothing arrives, there is no future time, and if nothing existed there would be no present time. Take the two tenses, past and future. How can they "be" when the past is not now present and the future is not yet present? Yet if the present were always present, it would not pass into the past: it would not be time but eternity.[10]

I tell my students that when they have difficulty in making progress while wrestling with a philosophical problem, progress can often be made by making a distinction. I think it will be very helpful here, as we grapple with the nature of time, to make a distinction. To begin to understand what I have in mind, let us make a further distinction between the Now and the Present.

[10] Saint Augustine, *Confessions*, trans. Henry Chadwick (Oxford: Oxford University Press, 2008), bk. 11, xiv, pp. 230–31.

In class, when I first introduce the distinction between the Now and the Present, I like to pause to savor the sight of students who either roll their eyes in disgust or stare in absolute bewilderment, wondering if they heard me correctly.

I give voice to the thoughts of the first group by saying, "Aha! This is why philosophy has such a bad reputation! It prides itself on hairsplitting distinctions between the 'Now' and the 'Present'!"

I give voice to the thoughts of the second group by saying, "Huh? How can there be a difference between the 'Now' and the 'Present'? Is that not like saying there is a difference between 'orb' and 'sphere'?"

I welcome the opportunity that the students have given me to show that subtle shades of meaning can have very significant differences. I ask, "Is there a difference between 'taste' and 'flavor'?" The students always yell, "No!" Then I tell them about a Polynesian restaurant I used to go to in Virginia, many years ago: "It is common in Asian restaurants for a note on the bottom of the menu to read, 'All Dishes Seasoned according to Your Taste.' At the bottom of the menu of this Polynesian restaurant were the words, 'All Dishes Seasoned according to Your Flavor'." There is usually a delay, and finally laughter as the light bulb finally comes on in their minds. I continue: "The moral of the story is—always pay very close attention to the meaning of words, even if the words do not seem to have immediately apparent differences." If we take the trouble to make a careful distinction between the Now and the Present, we will have a very powerful tool to use in our reflections on the nature of time.

The Now is time as a single point. It is the flow of moments unrelated to one another, each moment without any reference to a before or after. The Now is a self-contained immediacy. It is the temporal only in terms of a flash of existence, unrelated to before and after, without reference to past and future.

If the temporal could only be understood in terms of the Now, then life would be unintelligible. Let me offer an illustration. Before digital media, movies were stored on film. Each film was a stream of frames, depicting moment-to-moment transitions, stretching from beginning, to middle, to end. Imagine a film made up of frames from different movies. In such a film, one frame might be from, say, *Song of Bernadette* and the next frame from *Gone with the Wind* and the next frame from *Apocalypse Now*, and so on. Such a movie would be unintelligible, wouldn't it? It would literally be just flashes of nonsense. If the temporal were only the Now, reality would be experienced as one would experience that crazy film-of-unrelated-frames. To have any hope of understanding time properly, we must make a distinction and turn from the Now to the Present.

The Now is time as absolute immediacy; the Present is time extended; it is duration, that is, time in relation to a before and after. On this view, we may speak of Presents of varying durations, e.g., the present hour, the present day, the present semester, the present decade. The Present is bounded by origin (before; past) and terminus (after; future).

We may ask, "How far does the Human Present extend? Where are the bounds of origin and terminus that frame the Human Present?" To begin to address this question, we must make a further precision; we must speak of proximate origin and proximate terminus as well as absolute origin and absolute terminus.

The proximate origin of the human individual is conception, and the individual's (apparent) proximate terminus is death. What of absolute origin and absolute terminus? I want to be clear that I do not ask the question of absolute origin in evolutionary terms. In other words, I am not asking whether we are descended from apes or at what moment cavemen began to speak English. Likewise, I do not ask the question of absolute terminus in evolutionary terms. In other words, I am not speculating, in the manner of a science fiction writer, about whether mankind will evolve, say, to a higher form of consciousness and leave behind matter and travel as pure mind among the stars. What then do I mean, if not Darwin and Star Trek, when I speak of absolute origin and absolute terminus?

What I have in mind is the Human Present taken as a whole and extended as far back and as far forward as possible (analogous to an analysis in terms of antecedents and consequents). In other words, looking at the context of the real within which the Human Present occurs, how far back can we look at origins? Can we look back to a point before which there is no more before? How far ahead can we look at terminus? Can we look to a point after which there is no more after?

The accounts of the Human Present are decisively distinguished by how one accounts for absolute origin and absolute terminus. There are two alternatives, which are mutually exclusive. The first alternative I call the Closed System; the latter I call the Open System. Let's start with a very simple diagram to depict the Closed System.

Closed System

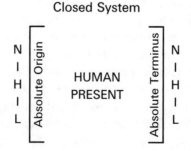

In the Closed System, the absolute origin of the Human Present is understood as a mere cosmic accident. Without designer or design, without purposer or purpose, the cosmos came into being; without designer or design, without purposer or purpose, conditions eventually came to pass from which humans arose. On this view, it would be better not to speak of a human nature, but rather of a human happenstance. That is, by sheer chance, elements of reality, over time, clumped together in a manner that resulted in what we now refer to as a human person, a being that is "the product of causes which had no prevision of the end they were achieving; that his origin, his growth, his hopes and fears, his loves and his beliefs, are but the outcome of accidental collocations of atoms."[11]

In the Closed System, the Human Present is bounded on the other side by an absolute terminus, which is cosmic collapse—complete and final cosmic collapse. ("No fire, no heroism, no intensity of thought and feeling, can preserve an individual life beyond the grave; that all the labours of the ages, all the devotion, all the inspiration, all the noonday brightness of human genius, are destined to extinction in the vast death of the solar system, and that the whole temple of Man's achievement must inevitably be buried beneath the débris of a universe in ruins.") This view of the Human Present, to borrow from Bertrand Russell, provides "the firm foundation of unyielding despair".[12] In evaluating the Closed System, I will consider the issues of time, death, suffering, ethics, and world view.

In the Closed System, human persons and the cosmos in which they reside are trapped in an inescapable hourglass;

---

[11] See the full quote from Russell below.
[12] Russell, *Mysticism and Logic*, pp. 47–48, as cited in John Hick, *Death and Eternal Life* (Louisville, Ky.: Westminster John Knox Press, 1994), p. 150.

moment by moment, the passage of time erodes personal and cosmic being. Each passing moment brings each and every person one moment closer to death and the cosmos one moment closer to cosmic collapse. In the Closed System, the adage "Patience is a virtue" must be dismissed as the statement of a lunatic. Patience is not a virtue for persons in a cosmos subject to collapse. Patience is a frittering away of finite and irreplaceable moments. What could justify patience? How could patience be anything other than a squandering of the limited moments available within a human life and within the cosmos? Said more colloquially, "Patience doesn't get you anywhere." (Of course, the astute observer will have already noticed that in the Closed System, *nothing* can "get you anywhere" because, in the long run, there is literally nowhere to go.)

Within our dark and lonely cosmos, pleasures are passing and pointless; suffering is an unredeemed and unredeemable misery. Death could be feared as an entrance into oblivion and the end of whatever pleasures one may have found; or, death could be welcomed as an entrance into oblivion and the end of whatever pains one may have endured.

What possibilities are available in the Closed System for morality and community? The best (if one could even use that word in this context) that one could do would be to achieve pleasure and avoid pain. Other humans could be an audience or competition or useful or something pleasant to rub against or a menace. Friendship, love, or altruism would be difficult to account for in the Closed System.

At the same time, there can be no evil in the Closed System. There may be the fact of pain in the Closed System (indeed, you can count on it!), but there cannot be what philosophers and theologians have called "the problem of evil". In its simplest form, the problem of evil asks: "How could an all-powerful, all-benevolent God allow evil in the world? If God is all-benevolent but cannot prevent evil, then he is not all-powerful; if God is all-powerful but will not prevent evil, then he is not all-benevolent."

We will deal with evil later in this work; but for now, I will simply point out that the "problem of evil" as a problem simply dissolves into meaninglessness in the Closed System. Evil is evil only if it falls short of a genuine standard of goodness. Absent an ultimate sanction, absent a transcendent and triumphant good—against which evil, as evil, is defined, measured, and judged—there is nothing truly praiseworthy or blameworthy—there can be no evil because there can be no good.

In the more thoughtless forms of science fiction, there is often a character who observes, "There cannot be good without evil." That is precisely backward. There cannot be evil without good. The Closed System precludes the possibility of good and, thereby, precludes the possibility of evil. There is certainly pain to be found in the Closed System, but *not* evil, because there is no possibility of fulfillment and approval, which possibility is essential for anything that could meaningfully be called "goodness".[13] As we shall see in our discussion of the Open System, raising the problem of evil as a *problem* demands and entails the triumph of good—or evil is meaningless.

Picture this: With every second that passes, you and the cosmos are moving to the abyss of nothingness as the absolute terminus. No matter what you do; no matter what you *do not* do—the result *must* be the same: cosmic collapse. Love or hate, mercy or revenge, kindness or cruelty, generosity or miserliness—*all* roads lead *inevitably* to

---

[13] For a more detailed account of this view of good and evil, see Errol Harris, *The Problem of Evil* (Milwaukee, Wis.: Marquette University, 1977).

personal and cosmic collapse. Whatever you do or do not do simply does not matter; whatever you do or do not do does not affect the final outcome, the absolute terminus, which is cosmic collapse. What would it do to a person to know that, not just notionally (i.e., "mere head knowledge", to use a phrase common to pop psychologists) but also affectively (not merely sentimentally, but at the roots of one's heart)?

Looking at the Closed System, let's ask: "Which world view would fit in best with the Closed System?" When I ask that question in class, my students immediately answer, "nihilism!" My reply always puzzles them: "Yes, but not yet."

The person in the Closed System is vulnerable. The etymology of that word is important. The Latin root of "vulnerable" is *vulnerare*, "to wound". To be "vulnerable" is to be "wound-able". The person in the Closed System is physically vulnerable. He is subject to hunger, sickness, and violence. He, like the cosmos, is also *existentially* vulnerable, that is, subject to cosmic collapse. Given his vulnerabilities, it would seem that espousing a world view of nihilism would be obvious, natural, inevitable. However, let's call to mind for a moment Elisabeth Kübler-Ross and her classic study of patients who had learned of their impending death. She said that they went through five stages of grief: "Denial, anger, bargaining, depression, and acceptance".[14]

Analogously, human individuals and communities, before "accepting" nihilism, would first go through Kübler-Ross' previous stages. Human individuals and communities would reject their vulnerabilities and convince

---

[14] Elisabeth Kübler-Ross, *On Death and Dying* (New York: Scribner, 2014), p. ix.

themselves that they had the wisdom, intelligence, virtues, and resources to secure themselves against their vulnerabilities. Trusting human reason (especially in the most exalted forms of a nearly divinized scientific method), human individuals would strive mightily to overcome or eliminate their physical vulnerabilities through the triumph of physical sciences and political arrangements. *Those* efforts would reinforce the world view of naturalism/modernism.

The persistence of the allure of naturalism is a cause for wonder. Even while two world wars were still in living memory, the sunny optimism of President Kennedy was able to captivate millions with an act of faith in human wisdom and self-sufficiency: "Our problems are manmade; therefore they may be solved by man.... No problem of human destiny is beyond human beings."[15] Fifty years later, great throngs happily joined together around another president and chanted, "Yes we can!" and "We are the change we have been waiting for!" That remains to be seen. My point is that the bleakness of nihilism is so obvious, the impotence of existentialism so certain, and the barrenness of postmodernism so undeniable that the wishful thinking at the core of naturalism returns as a hardy perennial. I suspect that blindness to present circumstances and the amnesia of the twentieth century help to sustain these world views that find a home within the Closed System.

The demise of the respectability of naturalism, found in the mounds of corpses and smoking ruins that pocked the twentieth century, led to what Kübler-Ross would call "depression", embodied in the stubborn defiance of

[15] John F. Kennedy, "Towards a Strategy of Peace", an address delivered to American University, Washington, D.C., June 10, 1963 (http://legacy.ford ham.edu/halsall/mod/1963Kennedy-peacestrat.html).

atheistic existentialism. The postmodernists, also unable to accept the full thrust and weight of nihilism, resort to irony, parody, detachment, and whimsy as a sufficient posture before the shadows cast by the vulnerabilities in the Closed System, all the while counting on the securities offered by electricity, direct deposit, tenure, and home delivery of the *New York Times*.

Naturalism, existentialism, postmodernism—all these are just one form or another of whistling past the cemetery. Each and all are equally futile. They are all forms of non-acceptance of the nihilism engendered by the Closed System. Is there any other account available to us of the absolute origin and absolute terminus of the Human Present?

Open System

```
E                                                    D
X                                                    I
N                                                    V
I                                                    I
H                                                    N
I    ←————— HUMAN PRESENT —————→    E
L                                                    
A       Absolute                Absolute       T
T        Origin                  Terminus      E
O                                                    L
R                                                    O
                                                     S
```

What of the Open System? In the Open System, the absolute origin of the Human Present is rooted in a transcendent exnihilating[16] agency—let it be named the Supreme Being, the First Cause, the Unmoved Mover, the Divine Artificer, the Purposer—the name is not of

---

[16] Referring to a cause that creates *ex nihilo*, that is, "out of nothing".

paramount importance inasmuch as I am simply presenting a conceptual framework.[17] I prefer to use the term "Exnihilator" because it expresses the function I have in mind and does not necessarily bring along with it all of the baggage associated with "God" or "Supreme Being". Nonetheless, some unpacking of the term is in order.

The act of exnihilation is the bringing into existence of that which did not exist before, without making use of any "ingredients" that existed prior to the act of exnihilation. People speak of making an apple pie "from scratch", by which they mean, say, that they made the crust themselves, rather than using a ready-made pie crust bought in a store. They do *not* mean that they brought the pie into existence from nothing. People who make pies, or anything else, act upon what already exists in such a way to bring about something else. No one who makes anything exnihilates.

What is so special about exnihilation? It is something with which we have no experience. From nothing, nothing comes. But in exnihilation, from nothing, *something* comes. Exnihilation, the progression from nothing to something, represents an absolute shift in category. Exnihilation, by which something is made from nothing, is an infinite act. That tells us a good deal about what an exnihilator must be like.

<hr />

[17] An interesting, if provisional, account of the Supreme Being as exnihilator can be found in Mortimer Adler, *How to Think about God: A Guide for the 20th Century Pagan* (New York: Macmillan, 1991). The reader would also do well to consider the more demanding and potentially more rewarding book *New Proofs for the Existence of God: Contributions of Contemporary Philosophy and Physics* by Robert J. Spitzer, S.J. (Grand Rapids, Mich.: Eerdmans, 2010). For an account of how a practicing scientist deals with "the God question", see Guy Consolmagno, S.J., *God's Mechanics: How Scientists and Engineers Make Sense of Religion* (San Francisco: Jossey-Bass, 2007), as well as his autobiography, *Brother Astronomer: Adventures of a Vatican Scientist* (New York: McGraw-Hill, 2000).

A being capable of an infinite act, as exnihilation is, must be infinite itself. As infinite, it lacks nothing; lacking nothing (unlike everything else in our experience), it must be a supreme being, having all perfections. That gives us an opportunity to pose a very interesting (and extremely important) question: *Why* would the Exnihilator exnihilate? (Said in more familiar terms: "Why would the Creator create?")

At first glance, it would seem that the Exnihilator has no good reason to exnihilate. Creation cannot add to the Exnihilator, which is infinite. A finite creation cannot perfect an infinite Creator. There is no way that the Exnihilator can benefit from what it has made. In that light, let's start putting some of the pieces of the puzzle together.

To be is good. (Metaphysics answers Hamlet's famous question with: "It is better to be than not to be.") To give a good, without any opportunity to receive benefit for having done so, is commonly called a generous act. The act of exnihilation is the zenith of generosity. It is a unique category of gift-giving; it is the giving of an absolute gift. In ordinary gift-giving circumstances, the recipient of the gift *already exists* and so is able to receive a gift. In exnihilation, the recipient of the gift is part of the gift that is given. It is brought into being from nothing. That which is exnihilated is the recipient of an absolute-gift of perfect generosity.[18] All of this has profound implications for the Human Present.

In light of the above, each human person, and the context of the real in which each human person resides, is the recipient of an absolute gift of supreme generosity.

[18] For an excellent and fascinating investigation of the generosity of creation, see Kenneth L. Schmitz, *The Gift: Creation* (Milwaukee, Wis.: Marquette University Press, 1982).

Let all of humanity look over its collective shoulder, so to speak, and look back at the common origin that each and all enjoy. All are rooted in a supreme benevolence. (How very different from looking back in the Closed System and seeing that man "is the product of causes which had no prevision of the end they were achieving; that his origin, his growth, his hopes and fears, his loves and his beliefs, are but the outcome of accidental collocations of atoms"!)

That man is the result of a deliberate act of benevolent exnihilation (creation) by an intelligent and benevolent Exnihilator (which, by definition, as infinite, lacks no perfection) means that man does indeed have a design, an essence, a *nature*, that neither he nor his society has chosen. The import and reach of that statement can scarcely be exaggerated. This statement, as we have already seen, flies in the face of existentialism and postmodernism. It is a contradiction of the anthropology of social reductionism, and it stands athwart all forms of ethical relativism. The nature of the absolute origin of the Human Present in the Open System has import for its absolute terminus as well.

In the Closed System, man, who is the result of the "accidental collocation of atoms" that, lacking intelligence, can have "no prevision of the end they were achieving", has no intrinsic purpose, no standard by which he may be judged to have succeeded or failed as a human. Maximum cosmic collapse is the final destination of each and all; therefore, there is literally nothing to look forward to, and what human individuals or communities do or do not do, in the end, simply does not matter.

The supremely benevolent Exnihilator, lacking no perfection, must also be intelligent, thereby capable of "prevision of the end" of what it has created. The Exnihilator, establishing the nature of a thing, is thereby the standard of its success or failure. More specifically, whether a human person succeeds or fails at being human is determined by the nature of the human, which is not made by the human. The mind and will of the Exnihilator, with prevision of the end of what it has created, are the arbiter of whether any human life has been lived in a manner worthy of the human nature with which each person has been endowed. The Exnihilator, supremely good, must also be supremely just and, therefore, must provide for the ultimate sanction, must provide for the rewarding for right and the righting of wrong. We will see in chapter 6 that a moral methodology that does not provide for a just and certain sanction cannot stand; it can only offer an ethics that cannot be lived.

Let me pause for a moment. In the preceding paragraphs, I have put down some very important philosophical promissory notes. I have made some dramatic claims about the consequents of the Open System. I invite, I *urge* the reader to reread this chapter after completing the book. Much of this chapter will not fully make sense until you have read the whole book. By the time you get to ethics, you will have a sense of the kind of metaphysical account that a sound and livable ethics demands. You must go back to this chapter and see if the account I am offering here is up to the job.

Greek philosophers spoke of the *telos*, the "purpose, end, fruition, accomplishment" of a thing. It is the root of the word "teleological", which is an essential term for our chapter on ethics. Aristotle used the term *entelékheia*, combining *enteles* ("complete, finished, perfect") and *ekho* ("to have"). In English, "entelechy" may be understood as an "intrinsic guiding force"[19] that moves a being toward its

---

[19] Robert J. Spitzer, S.J., with Robin A. Bernhoft and Camille E. De Blasi, *Healing the Culture: A Commonsense Philosophy of Happiness, Freedom and the Life Issues* (San Francisco: Ignatius Press, 2000), p. 49.

telos. For the human person and the human community, the *telos* they move toward is, metaphysically speaking, the absolute terminus, which is, morally speaking, the ultimate sanction that is the Exnihilator. In other words, humans, *rooted* in the transcendent, are also *oriented* toward the transcendent. Human entelechy, designed for and embedded within human nature by the Exnihilator, moves the human forward toward his proper *telos*; should the human achieve the end for which he was made, he succeeds, ultimately and fully, as a human. Should he not achieve the end for which he was made, he fails, ultimately and fully, as a human.

This point merits some further reflection. As an undergraduate, I changed majors, having started at college as a Spanish major and ending up as a philosophy major. Some of my students have changed majors more times than I can count, for reasons ranging from the wise and the prudent to the impulsive and the regrettable. In terms of your *humanity*, you cannot "change majors". You are always and irrevocably human. You may succeed as a human, and there is no more complete success than succeeding as a human. You may fail as a human, and there is no more complete failure than failing as a human. Those are the only options we will ever have. We get to choose, and choose we must and choose we do, whether deliberately or by neglect, but we do choose to succeed or fail at being human. More of what it means to be human we will see in the next chapter, on anthropology; what it means to succeed or fail at being human we will see in the chapter on ethics.

Picture yourself in the Open System, amidst the Human Present, at the bridging of past and future. Looking back over your shoulder, toward the absolute origin, you see that you are the result of a deliberate, transcendent, generous, providential act of creation. Think about what that means for human dignity—yours and that of your fellows.

Now look forward toward the absolute terminus. The future beckons you to fulfillment, satisfaction, the complete realization of the purpose of your human nature. At work within you is your human entelechy, the drive and momentum that reach across time from start to finish, urging you to lead a life that is worthy of your humanity. At that moment, how do you see time?

In the Closed System, as we noted before, the passage of time may be depicted as grains of sand passing through an hourglass. Each moment passing represents another step toward personal and cosmic collapse. The passage of time in the Open System, in contrast, is a "temporal unfoldment", as Tinder speaks of time throughout his book *Against Fate*.

On this view of time, we may borrow a phrase from Josef Pieper, who spoke of the human condition as *status viatoris*, that is, the "state of being on the way".

> It would be difficult to conceive of another statement that penetrates as deeply into the innermost core of creaturely existence as does the statement that man finds himself, even until the moment of his death, in the *status viatoris*, in the state of being on the way.... The state of being on the way is not to be understood in a primary and literal sense as a designation of place. It refers rather to the innermost structure of created nature. It is the inherent "not yet" of the finite being. The "not yet" of the *status viatoris* includes both a negative and a positive element: the absence of fulfillment and the orientation toward fulfillment.[20]

So understood, the human condition is that of the "viator", i.e., a wayfarer or a pilgrim. Human individuals and

---

[20]Josef Pieper, *On Hope*, trans. Sister Mary Frances McCarthy, S.N.D. (San Francisco: Ignatius Press, 1986), pp. 12–13.

human communities are not merely out for a stroll through time and space; no, humans have a journey to make, striving to overcome their individual and communal incompleteness by arriving at the *telos* and ultimate sanction of the absolute terminus of the Human Present.

With such a view of time, one can afford to be patient. If time is what you must go through in order to reach your *telos*, then patience is actually progress rather than erosion. This is so because patience keeps one on the path toward fulfillment, restrains one from making regrettable detours or deviations, and can even keep one from abandoning the trip entirely.

With such a view of time, suffering need not be the meaningless, pointless terror that it is in the Closed System. Rather, suffering and pain are given meaning (even, one might daresay, value and redemption) by being part of what one passes through on the way toward fulfillment. In fact, there may be times when sidestepping suffering might take one off the path toward fulfillment; a temporary avoidance of suffering might lead one to the catastrophic failure to arrive at one's *telos*.

Seeing the "not-yet" of their present condition, seeing too the prospect of fulfillment, aware of the impulse and momentum of entelechy, human individuals and human communities can behold the opportunity and obligation to live a life worthy of human nature. Their thoughts and actions may be guided by the virtue of magnanimity. The Greek root of magnanimity is *megalopsuchia*, which may be understood as "greatness of soul" or "the orientation of the soul toward great things".

A passing acquaintance with history, or even a few moments of honest self-examination, reveal to us that individuals and communities are not always the most zealous and clear-sighted pilgrims on the passage through time toward the fulfillment that is the hallmark of the Open System. We will see more clearly in chapter 6, on ethics, how and why we become misdirected, confused, or distracted along the way. For now, let's consider these propositions:

1. If the Closed System is the correct account of the Human Present, then there is no honest alternative to the world view of nihilism.
2. If the Open System is the correct account of the Human Present, then theism is the most obviously fitting world view.

If the Closed System is correct, well, then, there is nothing more to be said. What would be the point? Bear in mind, however, that the Closed System demands a constitutive materialism, which, as we have already seen, cannot stand.

On the other hand, if the Open System is correct, what are the consequents for accepting the truth of the Open System? And what are the consequents of rejecting the truth of the Open System? These are relentlessly, ineluctably important questions. To paraphrase Ayn Rand, "You can avoid reality, but you cannot avoid the consequences of avoiding reality."

Bringing together my vocabulary with that of Glenn Tinder,[21] we may say that the most decisive, determinative issue is this: Are we creatures, or are we accidents? Said another way: Are we the result of an act of exnihilation, or are we merely the result of "collocations of atoms"? If we are creatures and we accept our creaturehood, with all of its personal and communal antecedents and consequents, then we will have what Tinder calls "destiny". If

---

[21] Especially the first two chapters of his *Against Fate*.

we are creatures and we do not accept our creaturehood, with all of its personal and communal antecedents and consequents, then we will have what Tinder calls "fate".

Allow me now to present a few snippets from Tinder and then to tie them together:

A destiny is a demand coming from beyond one's immediate environment and even from beyond the world as a whole. This is indicated by the impression of cosmic unconditionality that the term conveys. To try to live according to a destiny is to resist the slovenly reduction of life to comfort and expediency that is encouraged by commercial and popular culture.[22]

Destiny is given by something beyond nature and society, something that may be referred to as "transcendence". This is a term with religious overtones, and I would not want these to be overlooked and neglected. We have our origin as destined beings—destined, rather than merely natural or social—in transcendence. Attitudes partaking of awe and trust are inseparable from the realization of this condition. Destiny, however, need not be given any particular creedal definition ... thinking of the source of our being as transcendent inhibits us from exaggerating the wisdom, power, and virtue of any human agency.[23]

[Destiny is] ... essential selfhood, enacted in time, and given by transcendence. Personal being is essentially bipolar, temporal in reality and transcendental in origin.[24]

Transcendence is the margin of mystery beyond everything we do know and can know.[25]

[22] Tinder, *Against Fate*, pp. 6–7.
[23] Ibid., p. 42.
[24] Ibid., p. 43.
[25] Ibid., p. 44.

A person unreservedly receptive toward transcendence
would regard his life gratefully rather than possessively.
Confronting death—one of the ways the transcendent
forces itself on us—a person would be as uncertain yet
hopeful as Socrates was before drinking the hemlock. In
trying by all means to live, we equate destiny with biological life and thus elevate death into an absolutely final fate.[26]

Destiny is paradoxical. It is given to us from a transcendent source and for a transcendent purpose; yet it is
chosen by us, a choice ratified by living in harmony with
that choice, through time. Destiny is a gift, yet it is also
an achievement, both of the individual and of the community, an achievement attained by persistent and patient
integrity. As we shall see in the next chapter, on anthropology, only the Open System secures the conditions of
possibility (the indispensable antecedents) for genuine
individuals and genuine communities. The moral consequents of the Open System we shall see in chapter 6.

After presenting the concept of destiny, I offer the students an illustration that they find instructive. I speak of
the "destiny train".

Destiny Train

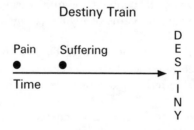

If one is acting in accord with the truth of the gifts, obligations, proscriptions, opportunities, and blessings of the
Open System, then one is riding the destiny train (powered

by entelechy). If one is not in harmony with the Open System, if one is not moving toward one's human *telos*, then one is acting "dysteleologically", *un*naturally (not "*un*natural" as "artificial", but *un*natural as *anti*-natural, that is, *against* nature). In such a case, one is "derailing" the destiny train. This can be readily illustrated by showing what happens when one wrongfully avoids pain or suffering that may be demanded by a moral life.

Destiny Train

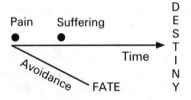

Let's say that you are married, and your spouse suffers an injury and requires a long stretch of care that is physically demanding and financially burdensome. It is quite easy to see that such a scenario will include pain and suffering. If you decide to avoid that scenario by abandoning your spouse, you may have avoided the trials of being a caregiver, but (as will be made clear in chapter 6) you will have derailed your destiny train by betraying your obligations to your spouse.

Joining Tinder's treatment of destiny with our understanding of the Open System, we have a useful set of tools for evaluating the quality of our lives as well as for evaluating the quality of communities, cultures, and civilizations. Looking at any of these, we may ask: "What is the direction of the train that we are on? Is it toward destiny (teleological) or not (dysteleological)? What is the momentum of the train? Are we really making progress?"

Now let's look at the other side of the coin. The opposite of destiny is fate, the consequent of rejecting creaturehood within the Open System of the Human Present.
Again, allow me to present a few strands from Tinder
and then to tie them together by means of my own set of
vocabulary and concepts:

> [Fate is] ... a term to designate all that assaults personal
> dignity. Fate is the impersonal and the antipersonal, per-
> vading time and space—determining events, and shaping
> society so comprehensively that there is no escape. Fate
> is present in all historical eras, but it is more dominant in
> some eras than in others.[27]

> At the core of my argument is the idea that fate is ironical:
> although it seems to come upon us from without, the truth
> is that we ourselves are the authors of our fate. Swept up in
> a drive to master the natural and social worlds, and ignor-
> ing the finitude and imperfection of man, we encounter
> human limits suddenly and disastrously. Fate is made up of
> the unexpected consequences of our own actions.[28]

Fate, as the rejection of the creaturehood at the core of
the Open System, is fundamentally dysteleological. It represents the human condition, writ large and small, at odds
with itself. Fate represents the consequences of rejecting
the human vocation, individual and communal, along
with all of its opportunities, obligations, proscriptions, and
gifts. It is the *Non serviam* ("I will not serve") of Milton's
Paradise Lost.

Fate is the naturalist's honest recognition of the physical and existential vulnerabilities of the human condition,
jaundiced and exacerbated by a rejection of the supernatural. With no alternative other than the vacuity of

[27] Ibid., p. 1.
[28] Ibid., p. 3.

nihilism, fate is the outcome of naturalism's attempts to provide the security that no finite human being, singly or *en masse*, can provide.

Fate is the existentialist's honest recognition of the physical and existential vulnerabilities of the human condition, jaundiced and exacerbated by a rejection of human life as a gift. With no alternative other than the vacuity of nihilism, fate is the outcome of existentialism's resolve to live as an orphan in the cosmos.

Fate is the postmodernist's honest recognition of the physical and existential vulnerabilities of the human condition, jaundiced and exacerbated by a rejection of reason and accountability. With no alternative other than the vacuity of nihilism, fate is the outcome of postmodernism's refusal to leave Peter Pan behind and finally grow up.

In need of the divine but refusing it, consigned to be a human subject but scorning it, humans under fate are the result of paradoxical attempts to be at once both a god and an object:

> The hidden link between the humanity and inhumanity of fate, then, is the inclination of each one to be something other than a mere human being: to gain the autonomy and transcendence of a god, or the irresponsibility and immanence of a thing. To be merely human is to live by bread which no social arrangements can absolutely assure; by faith and intellect, with all of the uncertainties inherent in both, and not by miracles which smother doubt; and in a state of freedom and, consequently, of anxious responsibility. It is not surprising that we recoil from circumstances as uncomfortable as these. In doing so, however, we give rise to the insubordinate events and powers that constitute fate.[29]

[29] Ibid., p. 19.

Tinder's work on fate and destiny is worth reading in its entirety. He interprets human history, man's relationship with nature, and social/civil life through the prism of fate/destiny. For our purposes, the categories of fate and destiny are particularly useful. In either case, the truth of the Closed System, or the truth of the Open System, the consequents are far-reaching. Opportunities and obligations are opened up or closed off, depending upon whether the concepts of the Closed System or the Open System offer a better account of reality. It does not take a great deal of cleverness or ingenuity to see that some of the darker chapters in human history can be well understood as the results of the rejection of the creaturehood that is the signal feature of the Human Present in the Closed System.

The categories of fate and destiny can be powerful tools for evaluating the antecedents and consequents for each layer of the Ethical Wedding Cake. They can help us to understand why, at the level of metaphysics, anthropology, and ethics, human life seems to be succeeding or failing. They can aid us in evaluating whether a philosophy or a polity will lead to human flourishing, will enable us to build a moral house in which we would want to live.

So armed, we are now well positioned to face the very difficult challenges of working out an adequate account of human nature, in chapter 5, on anthropology.

The 2 Dimensions of Metaphysics: Constitutive & Temporal

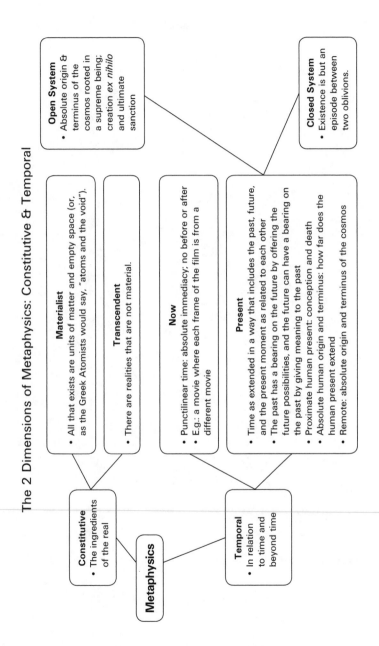

Metaphysics

Constitutive
- The ingredients of the real

Temporal
- In relation to time and beyond time

Materialist
- All that exists are units of matter and empty space (or, as the Greek Atomists would say, "atoms and the void").

Transcendent
- There are realities that are not material.

Now
- Punctilinear time: absolute immediacy; no before or after
- E.g.: a movie where each frame of the film is from a different movie

Present
- Time as extended in a way that includes the past, future, and the present moment as related to each other
- The past has a bearing on the future by offering the future possibilities, and the future can have a bearing on the past by giving meaning to the past
- Proximate human present: conception and death
- Absolute human origin and terminus: how far does the human present extend
- Remote: absolute origin and terminus of the cosmos

Open System
- Absolute origin & terminus of the cosmos rooted in a supreme being; creation *ex nihilo* and ultimate sanction

Closed System
- Existence is but an episode between two oblivions.

CHAPTER 5

ANTHROPOLOGY: AN ACCOUNT OF THE HUMAN PERSON

Know then thyself, presume not God to scan; The proper study of Mankind is Man.

—Alexander Pope

HAMLET: What a piece of work is a man, how noble in reason, how infinite in faculties, in form and moving how express and admirable, in action how like an angel, in apprehension how like a god! the beauty of the world, the paragon of animals—and yet, to me, what is this quintessence of dust? Man delights not me—no, nor woman neither, though by your smiling you seem to say so.

ROSENCRANTZ: My lord, there was no such stuff in my thoughts.

—Shakespeare, *Hamlet*

The following is an accurate account of a conversation I had with a student ...

STUDENT: I'm convinced that there is no significant difference between a human person and any other kind of animal. And I wanted you to be the first to know.

ME: I'm not convinced that you're convinced.

STUDENT: Huh?

ME: I'm not convinced that you're convinced that there is no significant difference between a human person and any other kind of animal, because you're talking with me and not a squirrel. Not only that, you wanted me to be the *first* to know—what difference would it make whom you told first if there were no difference between one animal and another?

There are some questions we simply cannot afford to get wrong, and among them is: "What is a human?" Philosophical anthropology is an attempt to offer a systematic and coherent account of human nature. In working out a sound anthropology, a philosopher faces such questions as: How is a human person like and unlike other kinds of beings? Is there really such a thing as human nature? Is human nature fixed, or does it change over time? Is any aspect of the human person not physical? How and why should a human person seek to integrate the apparently rational and nonrational elements of his life? What are the anthropological antecedents of human community? For humans, is death final?

These questions would be of concern for any sound anthropology. For our purposes, we will also address some other questions relating to human nature. This chapter is written in service of our larger project, which is to ground a robust and livable ethics, while also giving the reader a set of tools with which to evaluate moral claims. As we will see in this chapter and in the next, it is very easy to get it wrong and quite difficult to get it right. One of the reasons that working out a sound ethics is so difficult is, as was noted in the parable at the beginning of this book, that there are so many apparently irreconcilable elements to keep together: physical/non-physical; rational/nonrational; public/private; objective/subjective; law/freedom;

duty/love; habit/spontaneity; principle/praxis; fact/value; absolute/relative. While all of these will have to be reconciled in a sound ethics, most of them will have to be reconciled in a sound anthropology *first*.

This is the image I use in the classroom: It is not exceedingly difficult to juggle two or even three tennis balls. A few people can juggle four, five, six, or seven tennis balls, and fewer still can juggle so many for long. A philosopher who would offer a truly livable moral methodology would have to "juggle" many elements simultaneously and continuously. He can do it—with difficulty—if and only if he first learns how to keep coordinated ("juggle") many apparently irreconcilable anthropological elements.

Referring again to the Ethical Wedding Cake, anthropology provides antecedents for ethics. Anthropology provides the indispensable conditions of possibility for ethics. In other words, if you get anthropology wrong, you cannot get ethics right, except by chance. The anthropology you espouse will open and close doors for ethics. In this chapter, we are not simply working out anthropology for its own sake; we are working out an anthropology with an eye toward grounding a sound and livable ethics. As we make our way through this chapter, we should have these questions in mind: What does any ethics require of anthropology? (In other words, what must be true of the human person for there to be any talk of ethics at all?) What does a sound ethics require of anthropology? In other words, what does ethics require of anthropology if we are to build a moral house in which we would want to live?[1]

---

[1] By using the phrase "building a moral house in which we would want to live", I am not at all suggesting that morality is a social construct. Rather, I am saying that the formation of communities that lead to human flourishing arise neither inevitably nor accidentally, but emerge only through intelligent human effort, goodwill, and a clear vision of the nature and vocation of the human person.

To help us keep alert to the reach of such questions, let's bear in mind a question the reach of which is not immediately apparent: How is it possible to have a conversation? Said another way: What are the antecedents, the indispensable conditions of possibility, for two people to have a conversation about anthropology (or anything else)? I hope to show that if we keep *that* question at the forefront of our minds as we make our way through this chapter, discerning the merits of different accounts of human nature will be much easier.

Our treatment of anthropology will be in three parts. The first will look at various reductionisms (physical and social); the second part will look at dualism; the third will offer an account of a human person as a composition of bodily and non-bodily elements.

Recall our treatment of reductionism in our chapter on metaphysics. Reductionism is a "one-ingredient" account of whatever it is trying to account for. We saw that materialist reductionism results in an untenable metaphysics. The problem with reductionism is that it is an account that loses what it is trying to account for:

> Considerable emphasis in the intellectual world today is placed on attempts to understand what is familiar, experienced, or complex in terms of simpler, more precisely characterized units ... these are treated as alone real ... or are supposed to provide exhaustive explanation for whatever else occurs.... The result is a reductionism in which the originally acknowledged items no longer have any role.[2]

Whenever you hear someone say, "A human person is *just* ..." or "A human person is *nothing more than* ...",

---

[2] Paul Weiss, *Privacy* (Carbondale, Ill.: Southern Illinois University Press, 1983), p. 1.

then you know you are dealing with a reductionist. Let's not forget that it is very difficult—indeed, *impossible*—to be a thoroughly consistent and coherent reductionist. Reductionists are parasitic upon what they reject and make use of what they deny. The irony of reductionism is that if any anthropological reductionism were true, reductionists would be unable to tell you about it. Let's make that point clear by looking at physical reductionism first.

Put most simply, physical reductionism as an anthropology maintains that human nature can and must be explained only in physical terms: "Anthropology = Biology" or "Man = Animal" would be formulations of such a view. We have already examined the antecedents of this kind of anthropology in our previous chapter when we identified the insurmountable difficulties faced by materialism as a metaphysical account. At the heart of physical reductionism as an anthropology is the conviction that everything can be explained in purely natural, physical terms. This reductionism demands that metaphysical materialism be true. That demand puts anthropological physical reductionism on shaky grounds. Now, we will explore further the claims of this anthropology and then begin to draw out the reach and import of its consequences.

Let's go back now to the point I raised earlier about the conditions of possibility for having two people converse about anything at all. In class, I propose to the students the following thought experiment: How would two advocates of anthropological physical reductionism have a conversation about the truth of anthropological physical reductionism? On their own terms, would their conversation not have to be something like the following?

HUMAN #1 (*while pointing to his skull*): This brain is using this body to make noises ...

And then the conversation must break down. Physical and biological categories are not sufficient to maintain a conversation between these reductionists about reductionism.

Let's try the conversation again. This time I will underline key words.

HUMAN #1 (*while pointing to his skull*): This brain is using this body to make noises, <u>expecting</u> that that brain in that body over there will use the head to hear them. This brain is using this body to make noises, with the <u>intention</u> of enabling that brain in that body to <u>understand</u> this brain's <u>intended</u> and expressed <u>meaning</u> and <u>hoping</u> that that brain in that body will <u>infer</u> the <u>truth</u> of what this brain in this body is communicating. Furthermore, this brain in this body is <u>hoping</u> that that brain in that body will <u>agree</u> with the <u>truth</u> of the noises made by this brain using this body and then will signal <u>consent</u> to the truth <u>referred</u> to by this brain using this body.

Look at the words underlined: expecting, intention, intended, understand, meaning, hoping, infer, truth, agree, consent, refer. A physical reductionist must claim that all these words denote purely biological processes. In other words, expecting, hoping, intending, inferring, and the like can be reduced to arrangements of cells and chemicals. Such a view cannot answer the question, "*Who* is expecting, hoping, intending, inferring?" A lump of matter offering only a location of processes, a bag of nerve endings and appetites that can be tickled and fed—that is all that physical reductionism can offer. And it cannot even offer that. Does anyone really believe that truth can be detected by a body the way that salt can be tasted in a glass of water? Could such a belief be honestly maintained? How could truth be the concern of a brain? Can truth be detected the way that a conversation can be overheard?

The point of these questions is to show the fundamental flaw of physical reductionism as an anthropology. Physical reductionism, like all reductionisms, makes use of what it rejects. Anthropological physical reductionism refers to non-physical realities (e.g., truth, intention) to assert that there are no humanly relevant non-physical realities. In other words, if anthropological physical reductionism were true, there would literally be no one to have a conversation about its being true.

The key problem with physical reductionism as an anthropology is that "there's nobody home." There is no one, as Paul Weiss would say, "*living* the body". A body might make noises or "emit behaviors" (as I heard one psychologist say), but there is no person to infer, value, desire, hope, or act in morally significant ways. There can be no moral discourse because there is simply no one available to think about, much less converse about, morality. And there is no one who can both hear and evaluate as true or false the noises that might come from a merely biological human body. Physical reductionism cannot be a sound anthropology—much less is it an anthropology suited to undergird a sound ethics.

Social reductionism, by contrast, moves the anthropological emphasis from the human body to the human community. In other words, whereas physical reductionism claims that the human person is "nothing but" a body, social reductionism claims that the human person is nothing but various socially constructed roles in the context of community life. There is no objective reality that answers to terms such as, say, "human", "male", "female", "wife", "husband", "mother", "father", etc. These terms refer to roles that have no basis in nature but are rather products of will—they are socially constructed roles that human persons as actors adopt (consciously or not) and play. These various roles may be assumed, rejected, or exchanged as an actor might change masks on a stage.

As I write this chapter (summer of 2016), the social reductionist form of anthropology seems to be everywhere. "Gender" is now spoken of as being "fluid"; one can "identify" as "male" one day and "female" the next day and "neither" (*sic*) the day after.[3] Gender is simply a socially constructed role that one can choose to play various ways. Olympic decathlete Bruce Jenner now asks to be accepted as Caitlyn Jenner—and has received an award for doing so.[4] But this role-playing is more than a mere game. When journalist Ben Shapiro met "transgender reporter" Zoey Tur (formerly known as Bob Tur) and addressed Tur as "Sir", Tur put a hand on the back of Shapiro's neck and said, "You cut that out or you're going home in an ambulance."[5] Shapiro was threatened with violence because he did not play the role that another person wished to foist upon him.

Now, even racial identity is a "fluid" social construct. Rachel Dolezal, former director of Spokane NAACP, who in earlier photographs appears blonde, blue-eyed, and freckled, announced, "I identify as black"—later photographs of her suggest an altered appearance.[6] And

[3] "Girls Jealous after 'Fame' High School Crowns Boy Prom Queen", *New York Post*, June 26, 2016, https://nypost.com/2016/06/26/girls-jealous-after-fame-high-school-crowns-boy-prom-queen/.

[4] "Caitlyn Jenner Reveals ESPYs Acceptance Speech Insecurities", *New York Daily News*, July 20, 2015, http://www.nydailynews.com/entertainment/gossip/caitlyn-jenner-reveals-espys-acceptance-speech-insecurities-article-1.2298376.

[5] "Breitbart News Editor Ben Shapiro Files Police Report against Transgender Reporter", *New York Daily News*, July 21, 2015, https://www.nydailynews.com/news/national/ben-shapiro-files-complaint-transgender-reporter-tur-article-1.2298804.

[6] Greg Botelho, "Ex-NAACP Leader Rachel Dolezal: 'I identify as black'", CNN, updated June 17, 2015, http://edition.cnn.com/2015/06/16/us/washington-rachel-dolezal-naacp/.

therein lies the core of the problem of social reductionism as an account of anthropology—there are *only* (i.e.,
mere) appearances. There is the public, changeable face—
and nothing else. On this view, there is no actor with an
objective nature playing the role, wearing the mask. There
is only the role, only the mask, only the acting. But there is
no one playing the role, no one wearing the mask, no actor
who is acting. Yet we know that roles do not play themselves, masks do not wear themselves. There is no acting
apart from an actor. Someone must play the role; someone must wear the mask. *Who* is underneath the public
mere-appearance of the role, mask, acting? This question
social reductionism cannot answer. It can offer no answer
because on this view, there is "nobody home". There is
no enduring, self-identical agent with an objective nature
underlying the role, the mask, the acting. There is only an
asserted "identity" with no one to be identified.

Here we see that the physical reductionism and social
reductionism share two common flaws: one rather obvious; the other, less so. The obvious flaw both share is what
is true of all forms of reductionism, namely, that they make
use of what they reject. In asserting itself, each reductionism shows itself to be impossible:

> Reductionisms are parasitical on the data, observations,
> and confirmations of what they had presumably replaced.
> They presuppose that there are men who use their bodies
> as agencies for the realization of prospects which may have
> no bodily value. Each is offered as a truth for others to
> accept as a truth. All exist only so far as they at least tacitly
> cling to what was supposedly reduced, if only to provide
> the reductionists with a world in which they too can live
> and where their reduction can have a heuristic role.[7]

[7] Weiss, *Privacy*, p. 6.

The second and more subtle flaw that these reductionis-
tic anthropologies suffer from is that they both are dependent upon someone "being home", that is, an objective,
substantial, *truly personal* agent to make use of what they do
in fact accept. Physical reductionism depends upon a non-
bodily agency to make use of the body for non-bodily
purposes, e.g., to use the body to convey abstract truths or
work for goals that have no bodily import. Social reductionism depends upon an enduring, self-identical agent to
undergo the various "transitions" from identity to identity,
from socially constructed role to socially constructed role.
Social reductionism requires (even as it rejects) a private
person to wear the public masks that social reductionists
say constitute the human person.

*

To clarify the common, fundamental flaw in physical
reductionism and social reductionism as accounts of the
human person, we need to make some distinctions. I will
show that an essential distinction to make is one that dif-
ferentiates between (but does not divide) the public and
private dimensions of the person. Both reductionisms, in
addition to resting on the flaw of making use of what they
reject, also are flawed insofar as they fail to do justice to
the reality of and interplay between the public and private
dimensions of human persons.

Both forms of reductionism attend only to the public
dimension of the person and neglect the private dimension
of the person. In the case of physical reductionism, there
is acknowledged only the public dimension of the person that includes the body. Physical reductionism maintains that the human person is only the body—and thus
there is "nobody home". Therefore, because there is no

personal, private subject living the publicly available, objective body, there can be no accounting for human actions involving non-physical realities or purposes (such as striving toward truth).

Social reductionism has a similar failing. Social reductionism attends to the publicly available roles that the human person might play, but precludes the personal, private subject who would be needed to live out those roles. In other words, there is, again, "nobody home"—no subject to wear the mask and play the role.

Paul Weiss, in his book *Nature and Man*, gives us a vocabulary useful for properly distinguishing between the public and private dimensions of the person as well as an account of their essential interplay. In that work, he refers to the "outside" and "inside" of beings.[8] We will translate his words slightly and speak of the public and private dimensions of actualities, for reasons that will be made clear later.

Weiss in *Nature and Man* notes that each being has an inside. (This book was written in 1946. In 1977, he published *First Considerations*, wherein he refers to beings or substances as "actualities"—a term we will use in this work; in his book published in 1983, *Privacy*, he refers to the inwardness or the inside of an actuality as its "privacy" or what we call here its "private dimension".) Regarding the privacy or inwardness of an actuality, he notes that every actuality is something *on* the inside and is something *from* the inside. Did an actuality not have an *on* the inside, if it did not have a privacy, "it would be but an adjective, dependent for its nature and existence on something else, itself but an adjective of something further, and so on."[9]

---

[8] Paul Weiss, *Nature and Man* (New York: Henry Holt, 1947), p. 39.
[9] Ibid.

In other words, lacking a privacy, an actuality could not be itself. It is its privacy, its being something *on* the inside, that allows an actuality to say, "I have an identity—I am myself, and I am no another."

At the same time, an actuality is something *from* the inside. "It is a being with a characteristic perspective. Otherwise it would not express itself in an individual way. Each has an individual approach to what concerns it."[10] Being something *from* the inside, an actuality is capable of expressing itself in a privately initiated, publicly available manner.

Each actuality is also something *on* the outside. It is something with a public dimension. "It is a bounded reality, restraining the influence of other beings. Otherwise, it would be completely permeated by others and could not appear as a public distinct being." Absent a public dimension, or, said another way, were an actuality not something *on* the outside, it could not exist as something that could exist as other than all else and as something that is publicly available, something that could be found. (And let's not forget that people who cannot even find each other cannot have conversations about ethics.)

Each actuality is also something *from* the outside. As such, it is not only something "findable" (by virtue of being something on the outside), it is also something that once found can be taken account of and interacted with. As something *on* the outside, an actuality may say, "I may be found." As something *from* the outside, another may address an actuality and say, "I have found you and may interact with you."

Weiss concludes that an actuality "is an independent, individual reality, [encountering] and taking account of others. And it is all these at once. To suppose that any

[10] Ibid.

one, any pair or any triad of these exhausts the nature of a being is to divide the indivisible."[11] An insuperable difficulty with both physical and social reductionisms as the basis of anthropology is that they attend only to the public dimension of the human person. Physical reductionism attends only to the publicly available body, with no sense of the underlying, private agency necessary for the body to be lived, to be personified, to be used to express a private, non-bodily self and non-bodily concerns. Social reductionism attends only to the publicly available roles, with no sense of the reality or nature of the private agency necessary for the role to be played, for the mask to be worn. With the private dimension of the person precluded *a priori*, these reductionisms are, respectively, thereby incapable of accounting for the bodily actions and public expressions of actual human persons.

As this chapter unfolds, the explanatory power of Weiss' distinctions between the public and private dimensions of the human actuality and the distinctions regarding *from/on* the outside and *from/on* the inside will become more apparent.

*

Accepting that a "one-ingredient" approach to anthropology, i.e., that the human person is *only* bodily or *only* social, is untenable and that any anthropology that attends only to the public dimension of the person is unworkable, we turn now to a "multi-ingredient", multi-dimensional account of the human person. We need an anthropology that can account for both the public and private dimensions of a person—and so we turn to anthropological dualism.

[11] Ibid.

Weiss warns us that we must proceed with caution:

"The difficulty with a strict dualism of any sort is that it attempts to speak of two entities as completely sundered one from the other. If we have the one we so far do not have the other; yet we cannot know there are two unless we somehow have both of them together. Dualism says there are two exclusive positions, but in order to say this it must occupy a third position which includes them both."[12]

Dualism might be described as the separation of realities putatively together, but, on this view, divided by an enormous (perhaps unbridgeable) gulf. Let's first acknowledge that dualism may boast of an impressive pedigree in the history of thought. The dualism we meet today can trace its lineage through the centuries, back to Descartes of the modern era and Plato of the ancient world.

Over the centuries, we find that the result from these various dualisms has been a struggle to cross the chasm between one side and the other, between the public and the private, between the bodily and the non-bodily. Today we speak of "finding the other"; we ask how we can know whether there is anything "outside of the mind". Descartes in particular, in sounding the retreat from the body and its senses and the world around them (the public dimension) back toward his soul (the private dimension, the locus of the ego in his "Cogito ergo sum" [I think, therefore I am]) is at pains to account for how he could ever connect again with the world he left behind, a world the very existence of which he doubted. In response to these dualistic approaches, Weiss maintains that they point to a problem already solved—indeed, the problem never really existed. In the very raising of the question of dualism, the dualists

[12] Paul Weiss, *The World of Art* (Carbondale, Ill.: Southern Illinois University, 1961), p. 35.

show that the connection between what they thought was hopelessly distant already obtains in fact.

Dualism speaks of pluriformity (i.e., the public and private dimensions of an actuality) but cannot account for how the elements are together. It is an admission of defeat, rather than a discovery of fact, that the dualists insist that what they have been unable to account for as together must in truth be in separation.

Reductionism denies the existence of pluriformity. It is a confession of inattentiveness rather than a proclamation of astuteness that the assertion of reductionism makes use of what is familiar to deny what is being used.

Weiss lays the groundwork for a career-long objection to both dualism and reductionism. He overcomes the latter by showing that there are a diversity of elements and dimensions present in every actuality; and he will overcome the former by showing that there is continuity rather than a division between the elements and dimensions of each actuality.

Weiss maintains that the various dualisms are in fact already solved, because the very nature of an actuality precludes the kinds of divisions that have vexed the dualists for ages. Actualities are multi-dimensional, unified individuals who are together and interrelated with other actualities.

On this view, then, the oversimplifications of the reductionists are also precluded. The consideration of any one dimension of an actuality entails the consideration of the other dimensions. In other words, it is in the nature of an actuality to defy a uni-dimensional explanation.

The dualists, who divide what they distinguish and deny or cannot find the continuity of an actuality, dissolve their difficulties as they raise them. Whatever side they start on, they cannot wonder about what is, or how to get to, "the other side" unless actualities are in fact seamless. In other words, dualists are already in contact with what they claim they cannot find or reach or they would not be able to lament the separation from which they claim to suffer.

Dualism has the merit of trying to do justice to both the public and private dimensions of the human person. Dualism wants to acknowledge the locatable, identifiable public aspect of the person and wants to acknowledge the private individual who lives the public body. Unfortunately, a philosophical anthropology that starts with dualism inevitably falls into a hopeless solipsism.

The etymology of "solipsism" is revealing. Combining the Latin *solus* (alone) with the Latin *ipse* (self), solipsism is the state of being alone by oneself. One has no access to anything beyond one's self and has no reason or evidence to affirm that anything beyond the self enjoys extramental reality. Said more colloquially: The trouble with being a solipsist is that you cannot tell anyone about how right you are.

Perhaps an illustration here might help. Imagine receiving an invitation that reads: "*Please come to State College on Saturday, May 1, at 10 A.M. (EST), Founders Auditorium, to hear Doctor Smith's lecture entitled 'On the Non-Existence of Anything apart from My Mind'. R.S.V.P. via the Dean's office by April 24. Please reserve a space immediately so that we might have an accurate count for lunch. Valet parking available.*"

Such an absurdity, which is entailed by dualism, calls to mind historian Henry Brooks Adams' definition of philosophy: "unintelligible answers to insoluble problems."[13] Weiss would say that by simply asserting the problem of finding extramental reality, dualists have shown that there is no such problem.

---

[13] Henry Adams, *The Education of Henry Adams* (Boston: Houghton Mifflin Co., 1918), chap. 24.

In contrast with both dualists and reductionists, Weiss does justice to actualities, as they are in themselves and as they are together with others. Actualities are mysterious, yet knowable; knowable, yet never exhaustively known; publicly available, yet privately sustained; ineluctably private, yet accessible. What is the antecedent of this statement about actualities? In other words, what is the condition of possibility that must obtain in order for Weiss to overcome both dualism and reductionism?

The following is perhaps the most important statement in this work. I stress it daily with my students in all of my classes. I even joke with them about it, saying that although I tend to frown on tattoos, I might accept a tattoo declaring this principle: THE PUBLIC AND PRIVATE DIMENSIONS OF AN ACTUALITY ARE PERMEABLE.

What does this statement mean? What is the import of this statement? Why is it indispensable for our purposes? To say that the public and private dimensions of an actuality are permeable is to acknowledge that an actuality is one continuous being, multi-dimensional, yet unified. An actuality is, as was noted above, something *on the outside* and something *from the outside*; in other words, every actuality has a public dimension. At the same time, an actuality is something *on the inside* and something *from the inside*; in other words, every actuality has a private dimension. The public and private dimensions of a unified, complex actuality are in composition with each other—the dimensions are and must be distinguishable; the dimensions are not and can never be separable. The public and private dimensions of an actuality are in composition with each other, forming one unified being. Thus we call a proper anthropology, the only one adequate to a livable ethics, a composite anthropology.

*

What does ethics require of a philosophical anthropology? There are three functions and three relations that are indispensable to ethics. Without these, there can be no ethics at all—not even an inadequate ethics. As I lay these out, you will begin to see why physical/social reductionisms and dualism are incapable of grounding ethics. At the same time, I will offer a promissory note. Either the composite anthropology outlined here meets the demands of these functions and relations, or you should put this book down and just walk away.

We need an anthropology that does justice to the human person as solitary and social, always private and always accompanied, locatable yet hidden, publicly available while privately sustained. Such a human person is an embodied, intelligent freedom. Such a person is accessible without ever being able to be exhaustively known (and so may rightly be called "mysterious"). Such a person is multi-dimensional, rich, dense, and sacramental (in the philosophical sense of the word, which we will discuss later).

I stress to my students that ethics is impossible without the functions of responsibility, attributability, and accountability. I also alert that them to that fact that in ordinary conversation, the words responsible/accountable and responsibility/accountability are used interchangeably. We have all said, and we have all had said to us, "I'm holding you responsible!" as well as, "I'm holding you accountable!" Using these words interchangeably is an imprecision that does not serve us well. We will maintain the distinction between the two in the following manner.

Responsibility refers to my power to initiate privately, that is, *from the inside*, actions that are publicly available, that is, *on the outside*. In other words, "responsibility" refers to my power to be the source of my own actions. "Responsibility" refers to my ability to say, rightly, "I did it." I inwardly initiate my outward actions.

In the classroom, students in the front row become my props to illustrate philosophical points. To illustrate responsibility, I take a swipe at a student and say, "Suppose I whacked George here in the forehead. What would you think if, after doing so, I looked at my hand and said, 'I wonder why the atoms of that hand did that? Why would the atoms of that hand want to hit George?'" The students chuckle and see my point. I continue: "No! *I* hit George! I made a private, inwardly initiated choice as a moral agent to use *my* hand to strike him—in order to express my deeply held conviction that hats should not be worn in the classroom."

How is it possible that *I* can make use of my hand to express my self and my conviction about hats in the classroom? Reductionisms cannot account for this; as we have seen, they only account for the public dimension of the person. There is no private source that can initiate publicly available, morally significant action. Dualism cannot account for this action, either; dualism, devolving into solipsism, cannot find extramental reality, and so the person has no access to the public dimension for public action.

This brings us to the Permeability Principle ("The public and private dimensions of an actuality are permeable"). Because the boundary between the two is permeable, I as a moral agent can move beyond my privacy, acting into the public dimension, so that my publicly available actions become attenuated expressions of my inner private self.

With responsibility (and its dependence on the Permeability Principle) so understood, we can turn to attributability. The function of attributability is to address a moral agent as the source of an action and say, "*You* did it." The function of attributability makes my tongue-in-cheek question, "I wonder why the atoms of this hand hit George?" appear ridiculous, and rightly so. Attributability allows a person to trace a publicly available action back to me as its private, responsible source. Again, the condition of possibility for this moral attribution is the Permeability Principle. Attributability allows one to note that while my body is the instrument of my action, *I* am the initiating source of that action. In other words, the Permeability Principle enables attributability to link, in a morally significant way, public actions to a person with a privacy. So understood, we can turn now to consider accountability.

Accountability has three steps. The first step of accountability is to ask the agent, "Why did you do it?" The person asking the question is seeking to ascertain if there is moral justification for the action. In the second step, the agent responds with an explanation: "I did it because ..." In the final step, the person asking, "Why did you do it?" evaluates the explanation and then assigns a sanction, that is, assigns praise or blame to the moral agent as the responsible, privately initiating source of the publicly available action. Note that this interaction of "Why?", "Because ...", and praise/blame is possible because of the Permeability Principle. Other people are able to observe my actions, attribute my actions to me, and hold me accountable for my actions only because there is continuity between the public and private dimension of the human person.

Without the functions of responsibility, accountability, and attributability, there can be no ethics of any kind. The antecedent, the condition of possibility for these three functions, is the Permeability Principle. A consequent of this fact is that only a composite anthropology can ground any ethics, because only a composite anthropology is in harmony with the Permeability Principle.

Another way to express the import of permeability for anthropology and ethics is to state: "I am always more than just my body, but my body is where you can begin to find me." This statement is not only relevant to the three functions of ethics described above; it is also indispensable for accounting for three essential relations that must be accounted for in a sound ethics, namely, I-It, I-You, and I-Thou.

The relation of I-It is a relation of person to object. There is a sense in which a person may be rightly considered an object. For example, if I am a pilot of a small airplane, it matters not, in terms of aerodynamics, whether the plane is loaded with 150 pounds of bananas or 150 pounds of you—what matters is the weight of 150 pounds. As an object, a person is locatable in time and space, has dimensions and qualities, etc. A person, however, is never merely or solely an object (a fact that reductionism cannot account for, by the way). The relation I-It attends to the objective dimension of the person, without any reference to the private dimension of the person; it acknowledges the human body as a physical body only, as an object, but not as a distinctively *human* body being lived and used by a human privacy, as a whole person. A sound ethics that does justice to a sound anthropology must address the relation of I-You, that of my relation to you as a human subject, a moral agent. Acknowledging such a relation and acting accordingly is a matter of justice. To do otherwise would be unjust, an inadequate response to the person present to me.

With the relation of I-You, I attend to you with particular reference to your distinctively human privacy. Contrary to physical reductionism, the I-You relation insists that you are more than just a body, even while insisting that you have one. Contrary to social reductionism, you are more than just the social roles you may play, even as you play them. Acknowledging the demands of composite anthropology, I acknowledge you as a morally significant human being, as a moral agent, as an actuality whose being and humanity are continuous from the public dimension to the private dimension. Perhaps an illustration will help clarify the morally indispensable distinction between I-It (person-as-object) and I-You (person-as-subject) relations.

In class, I will approach a student and ask, "Suppose I stick my finger in George's eye. What have I done? In terms of the I-It relation, I will have *injured* the eye of that body—a matter of physical significance. In terms of the I-You relation, I will have *wronged* the person, George—a matter of moral significance. And if George and I had, until very recently, been the best of friends, in terms of the I-Thou relation (the person of George as not any person but as a friend, as an intimate, as a unique individual), I will have *betrayed* my friend George—a matter of grave moral significance." I am delighted when I see the students nod in recognition. How can they discern this profound truth so readily?

Well, it is common sense; it is consistent with ordinary human experience, including the experience of the students. They also readily perceive the truths pointed to by the illustrations because they understand the Permeability Principle. They know that these three relations (I-It, I-You, I-Thou), with which they have lived their whole lives and without which truly human life is impossible, are rooted in the continuity of the human person from the outermost reaches of the public dimension (the human body, as something *on the outside*, approachable *from the outside*) to the innermost reaches of the private dimension (the human privacy, as something *on the inside*, expressing itself *from the inside*).

Let's consider now in more detail how a composite anthropology, grounded upon the Permeability Principle, works. To do so, let's have a look at the illustration below, which I call the Funnel Concept of the Body.

Funnel Concept of the Body

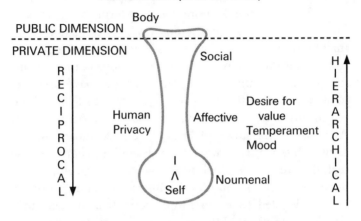

Some students, upon seeing the diagram for the first time, note the resemblance between the diagram and a type of beer glass known as the "half-yard glass".[14] That glass, in fact, was the inspiration for the diagram, as the shape of the glass models well what I wish to depict about the human person—his body and his privacy.

The outermost rim of the funnel is the locus of the human body. It is the attenuated expression of the person into the public dimension. As I remind my students frequently, "I am always more than just my body, but my body is where you may begin to find me." What else is there besides the human body? The "interior" of the glass[15] is the private dimension of the person—the human privacy.

I suppose I should pause here and explain why I am following Weiss' example of using the term "human

---

[14] https://images-na.ssl-images-amazon.com/images/I/41mTsvOr8sL._SL500_AC_SS350_.jpg.

[15] Please note that the spatial metaphors are just that—metaphors. You cannot observe the human privacy by looking down someone's throat or into his ear.

privacy" to refer to the non-corporeal aspect of the person. Why not use a more familiar term, such as, say, "soul", "mind", or "consciousness"? These latter terms may be more familiar (insofar as they are used frequently today), but they are not at all more obvious in their meaning. Different thinkers over the centuries have used the same words in different ways. If we speak of "soul", do we mean "soul" as used by, say, Plato? Or Aristotle? Or Aquinas? If we speak of "mind", do we mean "mind" as used by, say, Descartes or by Freud? Rather than use technical terms weighed down by long, convoluted histories, subject to countless qualifications and footnotes, I have decided to use a simple term that answers to a simple description. "Human privacy" refers to the private dimension of the human person, that which a person is, using Weiss' formulation, "from the inside".

Looking at the base of the funnel, we see that the root identity of the person is the self. The outward-facing aspect of the self is the I. (So understood, we can see more clearly the import of the statement "I use my body to express my self.") Moving up the length of the funnel, we note layers of the privacy. Not compartmentalized, the boundaries between these layers are permeable. Those located toward the bottom of the funnel represent the more hidden (but not necessarily inaccessible or unknowable) aspects of the privacy; those closer to the top are closer to the public dimension and the body and are more associated with the body for expression.

At the lowest level we see the "noumenal". I struggled for years to find an appropriate word to describe this deep layer of the human privacy. I am not entirely satisfied with my choice, but it is at least defensible. "Noumenal" is related to the Greek word *nous*, which is suggestive of the English word "mind". In this case, by "noumenal" I am referring to what in the Western tradition would be recognized as the "powers of the soul", that is, reason, will, and memory. It is the organizing principle of the human privacy.

Immediately above that is the "affective". I use that word in three senses, and each sense has a role to play in moral development and moral evaluation, as we will see later in this chapter and the next. In the first sense, by "affective" I mean "appetite-for-value" or "desire-for-value". That term immediately requires explanation, lest it be inferred that I am advocating some form of ethical emotivism.

According to ethical emotivism, if I say, "Abortion is wrong", what I am *really* saying is "I don't like abortion" or "I don't like how I feel when I think about abortion." When I say, "Democracy is good", what I am *really* saying is "I like democracy" or "I like how I feel when I think about democracy." On this view, moral evaluation is simply a declaration of my emotional preferences and state at any given moment. It is a form of ethical relativism.[16] This is certainly *not* what I mean when I speak of the affective as a "appetite-for-value". Rather, I intend to connote a combination of empathy, sympathy, and compassion. It is a capacity to respond to the presence of moral worth beyond an exclusively rational calculation of price and utility. It is at once an appetite for the good and a sensitivity to the presence of what is judged to be of moral worth.

The second sense of the affective is that of "mood". I contrast it with the third sense of the affective, which is that of "temperament". Both mood and temperament are important because they can greatly influence moral

---

[16] For a brief yet thorough thrashing of ethical relativism, see Francis Beckwith and Gregory Koukl, *Relativism: Feet Planted Firmly in Mid-Air* (Grand Rapids, Mich.: Baker Books, 1998).

sensitivity and action. I explain to my students the difference and relation between mood and temperament by means of an analogy: "Mood is to temperament as weather is to climate." Mood, like weather, is subject to rapid change. It may be raining one moment and dry the next. In terms of mood, you might be sad one moment and enraged the next. Temperament, like climate, is more or less stable. I have lived in Southwest Florida, where, according to the old joke, the three seasons are, "Hot, Very Hot, and You've Got to Be Kidding Me!" It might get as cool as 45 degrees Fahrenheit in late December, but you will not ever see snowdrifts in Southwest Florida. You can count on the climate to be tropical, within a very predictable and stable range. Likewise for temperament—some folks seem to be nearly constantly optimistic; I myself tend toward the pessimistic and the gloomy (e.g., "Not only is the glass half-empty, it is leaky and resting on a rickety table").

Above the affective, and nearest the body and the public dimension, is the "social" layer of the human privacy. The social refers to the human capacity for communication and human interaction. It is most likely to make use of the human body in more publicly available ways, such as speech, gesture, etc.

Note the arrows on either side of the funnel depicted above. These arrows illustrate the bi-directional relationships that obtain among the layers of the human privacy and the public and private dimensions of the human person. The arrow on the right of the diagram runs from bottom to top, indicating a relationship among the layers and dimensions that I refer to as "hierarchical". The arrow on the left of the diagram runs from top to bottom, indicating a relationship among the layers and dimensions that I refer to as "reciprocal". Let's start with the hierarchical relations first.

"Hierarchy" refers to a system wherein the elements are ordered by rank. How does this apply to the human privacy? That which is closer to the public dimension is less essential to my identity as this particular, unique human person. That which is closer to the public dimension is more easily changed. That which is deeper in the privacy, that which is closer to the root of identity in the self, is progressively more intimate, individualized, unique, and enduring. The deeper levels of the privacy use the other layers and the body for the sake of self-expression. The deeper levels of the privacy give rise to and govern the other layers of the privacy as well as the publicly available body.

If the hierarchical describes the relations from the root of the private dimension of the person to the rim of the person at the public dimension (the body), the reciprocal describes the relations in the other direction, from the public dimension to the private. We can see this easily if we recall the relations of I-It, I-You, and I-Thou. When I spoke of sticking my finger in a student's eye, I noted that, in doing so, I have injured his body (I-It); I have wronged him morally as a person (I-You); and, if we had previously been friends, I have betrayed him as a friend (I-Thou). In other words, actions in the public dimension can reach "down" into and affect the human privacy.

Note that neither anthropological reductionisms nor dualism can account for hierarchical or reciprocal relations. Physical and social reductionisms cannot do so because there is nowhere for relations to go—they each account for, in various ways, a different aspect of the public dimension of the person. Anthropological dualism cannot account for these relations, either, as it so divides the dimensions that it is at pains to establish a bridge between them. Consequently, the solipsist that is the inevitable result of dualism is incapable of self-expression (the hierarchical relation) and is incapable of being affected by anything not himself (the reciprocal relation).

Having drawn out the workings of the human person in terms of both hierarchical and reciprocal relations, let's look more closely at the interplay between the public and private dimensions of the person, in order to understand better interactions between persons, which are an indispensable element of ethics.

*

To achieve a better understanding of interactions between persons, we will make use of the categories of sign, symbol, and sacrament. I expect that there will be no objection to making use of the categories of sign and symbol in order to talk about the human person—but what about sacrament? Is sacrament not an exclusively theological category? Does having recourse to the category of sacrament not make this anthropology a distinctively Catholic anthropology and thereby irrelevant, or at least inaccessible, to many Christians as well as to non-Christians, especially agnostics and atheists? Not at all.

Let's review what we said earlier about the intersecting model of faith and reason. Reason can interrogate faith and can ascertain whether faith's propositions are intelligible (that is, not nonsensical), even if reason is unable to ascertain whether or not a given proposition of faith is true. For example, philosophy can talk quite helpfully and clearly about "nature" and "person", even if it cannot verify or falsify the classical Christian definition of Christ as having two natures (human and divine) in one Person or the Trinity having three Persons (Father, Son, and Holy Spirit) in one divine nature. A philosopher can converse with theology without necessarily thereby becoming a theologian. Likewise, a philosopher can make use of categories of theology for their explanatory power, without necessarily making an act of faith.

Let's begin with a treatment of sign, move on to symbol, and then make use of the category of sacrament. In the last instance, we will be especially alert to stay within the bounds of philosophy, even while making use of a theological category.

A sign is an indicator. It points away from itself to what is signified. I tell my students that when I want to leave the building, I do not stand under the exit sign and say, "Look! I've left the building!" To leave the building, I must go to where the exit sign points. Likewise, if I want to have lunch on campus, I do not stand under the cafeteria sign and ask, "Where's the food?" No, I go to where the sign points—which is to the cafeteria, where the food is.

A symbol is a kind of a sign. Like a sign, it indicates, that is, it points to something not itself, but it is also much more than a sign. A symbol is a kind of mediator—it stands between the public and private dimensions. It stands between that which is symbolized by the symbol (the symbolized resides in the private dimension) and the reader of the symbol (the reader is found in the public dimension). The symbolized uses the symbol to draw the attention of the reader to itself. An illustration at this point may be useful.

Immediately after my parents were married, they moved into the apartment on the second floor of the house owned by my mother's parents, who lived on the first floor. Shortly after coming back from their honeymoon, my parents were going out to dinner. My grandfather yelled at my father, his new son-in-law, as he had done when my parents were still dating. He said, "You bring my daughter home at a decent hour!" My mother did not say a word to her father. Instead, she held up her left hand and, with her right hand, pointed to her wedding ring. My grandfather shrugged his shoulders and replied somewhat sheepishly, "Sorry, ... force of habit."

What happened? How did my grandfather understand what my mother "said", when she did not say anything? How did she communicate so effectively and convincingly without words? To understand what happened in the story above, we have to pause for a moment and reflect on the nature of signs and symbols.

A sign is noteworthy only insofar as it points to what is signified. What is signified is more important than the sign. A symbol is a kind of sign. Like a sign, it indicates, it refers to another—in this case, the symbol refers to that which is symbolized. The symbol is a mediator. It is a bridge between that which is symbolized and the reader of the symbol. Unlike the relationship between the sign and the signified, the relationship between the symbol and the symbolized is more profound and more intimate. There is continuity between the symbolized and the symbol. We may view the symbol as an attenuated expression of the symbolized.

Going back to the story of my mother and her wedding ring, we can see that the ring is a symbol of the marriage. The marriage, the bond between my mother and father, is in the private dimension—it is neither visible nor tangible. Nonetheless, symbols of its reality are publicly available. We might say that the marriage uses the ring to say, "Here I am!" The privately subsisting reality that is the symbolized uses the publicly available symbol to announce itself. A competent reader of the symbol rightly acknowledges the symbolized that expresses and announces itself through the symbol.

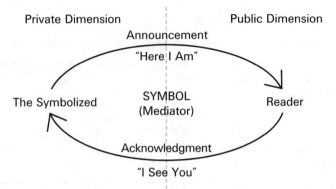

So understood, we can see why the communication between my mother and grandfather, though nonverbal, was immediate and convincing. The ring was an effective symbol—an annunciation, if you will—of that which was symbolized, namely, the marriage. My grandfather was a competent reader of the symbol and acted accordingly.

Recall that earlier in this work, we reflected on the relationship between faith and reason. One of the reasons we did so can be seen here. We need to move beyond signs and symbols to make use of the category of "sacrament" as a means of understanding the human person, the relationship between the physical and non-physical, private and public dimensions of the person and the interactions between persons. We can make use of the illustrative and explanatory power of the category of sacrament without having to pronounce on the truth or validity of sacraments such as baptism, etc., for pronouncements on such matters are the work of theology and not philosophy. As philosophers, if we avail ourselves of the category of sacrament, we have a means of illustrating the composite nature of the human person and thereby offer a coherent account of philosophical anthropology not to be had by other means.

A sacrament is a kind of a symbol. Like other symbols, a sacramental symbol is a mediator between the symbolized and the reader of the symbol. The difference lies in the fact that a sacramental symbol is a symbol taken up *in action*. In the administration of sacraments, for example, water is poured, bread and wine are offered, etc. Like an ordinary symbol, the symbolized announces its presence by means of the symbol. The proper response of the reader of the symbol is to acknowledge the presence of the symbolized that the symbol announces. In sacramental action, the symbolized not only announces itself to the reader; it also invites the reader to come into contact with the symbolized through the sacramental action.

While the response of a competent reader of an ordinary symbol is simply acknowledgment of the reality of the symbolized that is made public by the symbol, the proper response to a sacramental symbol taken up in action is much more complex and rich. The response of the competent reader to the invitation offered by the symbolized through the sacramental symbol is one of self-donation. In response to the symbolized saying through the sacramental symbol, "Here I am!" and "Come to me!", the reader of the symbol responds with, "I give myself to you." The competent reader of the sacramental symbol uses the sacramental symbol in action as a medium to pass through the attenuated self-expression of the symbolized through the symbol to the very symbolized itself. The competent reader's passage through to the symbolized by the act of self-donation in response to the invitation is a contact between the reader and the symbolized, leading to a transformative communion of the reader with the symbolized. I hope that the diagram below will begin to make this dynamic clear.

Sacramental Symbol in Action

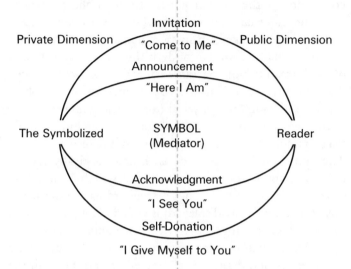

Keeping an eye on the diagram above, let's illustrate the sacramental dynamics with an example of human interaction. Years ago, I was asked, "Why does your medical ethics class spend so much time talking about sexual matters?" I answered: "Because sex is a comprehensively human issue—it leaves out no aspect of human nature. Consequently, if your moral methodology gets sex right, then nearly every other moral matter falls into place. If your moral methodology gets sex wrong, then there is little of moral significance that you can get right." Accounting for a composite anthropology through the category of sacrament, we can develop a moral methodology of great explanatory power.

The above statement will become clear if we recall the Permeability Principle that we spoke of earlier: "The boundaries between the public and private dimensions of an actuality are permeable." Let's link that insight into the continuity of the human person from public to private with our understanding of the link between the symbolized and the symbol taken up in sacramental action. My contention is that the human body is the sacramental symbol of the human person. Sacramental action allows the invisible (the private dimension) to become visible (publicly available) through the physical (the public dimension).

In a sexual encounter, the nakedness of the human body is a sacramentally symbolic revelation of the private person. The "unveiling" of the body is anthropologically significant. In many religious traditions, that which is sacred (in other words, that which is not merely ordinary, not merely physical and publicly displayed) is veiled. The unveiling of the sacred is a solemn act that takes place under very precise conditions, conditions set in order to announce and secure the integrity and dignity of the sacred symbol beneath the veil. The beholding of the sacred unveiled and revealed is a privilege granted only to those who have met precise (and often demanding) conditions. If the veil is simply yanked off the sacred symbol, then that which is symbolized is not properly revealed (and remember that true revelation is a gift—a "grace") but rather merely exposed. In that case, the sacramental symbol is displayed as a mere object, and the sacral character of the symbolized is cheapened (it costs nothing to see it) or even obscured.[17] On this view, seeing the naked body of another person is a privileged gift that must be earned through the commitment of marriage.

In sexual intercourse, the individual is reaching out from his core identity and, if you will, pouring out his privacy

---

[17] One could use these reflections as a point of departure for reflecting on the anthropological and moral import of modesty in dress, as well as the turpitude of pornography.

through his public body—the noumenal, the affective, the social, the physical—and, at the same time, is receiving the person through the body, receiving the import and meaning and distinctiveness and uniqueness of the person.

Aletheia is the Greek word for "truth". It is a combination of the "privative" prefix *a-* (signifying lack, absence, or negation) and the Greek word *lethe*, meaning forgetfulness (therefore making truth a lack of forgetfulness, or un-forgetfulness). The word is said to derive from *letho* or *lanthano*, meaning to escape notice or to cause to forget, together with the alpha-privative prefix, which negates the idea. On this view, truth (or perhaps, better said, "truthing") is a process of disclosing or un-concealing what is hidden. Related to our reflections on anthropology, the truthing of the person is a making available or "publicizing" the otherwise hidden private self of the person through an unveiling of the human body. So understood, a truly human sexual encounter can never be "just sex" or a merely, solely biological encounter or just a friction-induced release of endorphins. On the contrary, a truly human sexual encounter is always a great metaphysical and anthropological dramatic event, a sacramental action of great moral import.

Let's reflect on a few more aspects of sacramental dynamics. If we do so, we can enrich our philosophical anthropology and from there establish some moral compass points by which we may more safely navigate sexual ethics.

We will start by reflecting on the distinction between the profane and the sacred. One Latin word for "temple" is *fanum*. That which is profane is that which is before or outside of the temple. Something becomes sacred when it is brought inside the temple. More specifically, something becomes sacred when it is placed on the altar for sacrifice. In common usage, "sacrifice" connotes the killing or destroying of an offering given to the divine. But the term has denotative dimensions as well. The Latin *sacrificium* is derived from *sacrum* (sacred) and *facere* (to make). To sacrifice something is to make it holy, to set it aside for divine purposes by placing it upon the altar, reserving it for a not-profane use.

Let's look at a concrete example. A gold cup, for instance, can be an admirable work of art as well as a suitable drinking vessel. It becomes a sacred vessel when it is placed on the altar in a temple, thereby designating it for sacred (that is, not-profane) use. It is *profaned*, that is, used in a manner contrary to its dedicated divine purpose, if it is later employed for merely ordinary use as a drinking vessel.

I would make this point in class in the following way: "Suppose I hand you the chalice I use for Mass and say, 'It's late in the afternoon and I'm running out of energy—take this to the cafeteria, fill it with coffee, and bring it back to class for me.'" The students said they would refuse. "But why? It doesn't leak. It has a broad base, and so it is not prone to tipping over. It is well suited for holding coffee." In various ways the students would insist, "But that's not what it's for! It has been dedicated to a divine purpose. Use a profane vessel for a profane purpose and use a sacred vessel only for a sacred purpose."

Their insights into the nature of sacred vessels are worth reflecting on, for the insights can illuminate the particular character of a composite anthropology and provide resources for a moral methodology adequate to the task of guiding a worthy sexual ethics. Acknowledging the human body as the sacramental vessel of the human person is equivalent to acknowledging that the human body is the public expression of the private person. This acknowledgment is significant both anthropologically and morally.

With a person so described, the human body cannot be a mere object and, morally speaking, ought not be treated as the other half of an I-It relationship. Morally speaking, the ethical minimum must begin at the level of an I-You relationship between any persons. The human body, because of its sacramental relation to the human person, ought not to be used "profanely" (say, as a mere instrument for pleasure) but must be treated in accord with its sacred, sacramental character. In fact, we will see later that because of the revelation of the person through the naked body is so profound, and the expression of the person through the body so intimate, we may say that the uniqueness of the person is made available in a sexual encounter. Consequently, the sexual encounter may only be rightly understood as an I-Thou relationship and must be morally evaluated as such. Later on, we will reflect on the moral import of the comprehensive scope of self-disclosure/self-donation in the sexual encounter.

Let's think some more about the distinction between the sacred and the profane and about the distinctive character of the sacramental symbol. My students (including non-Catholic students) had an intuitive grasp of the import of the sacred character of the sacramental vessel. Even though a Mass chalice could be useful as a coffee mug, they recognized that it had a higher purpose and status. To use it in a way that is inconsistent with its higher purpose and status is to dishonor, to misuse, to *profane* that which has been set aside for a distinctive sacred purpose. In other words, the sacramental symbol has a meaning and proper use that we ourselves can acknowledge but that we ourselves do not decide. Thus, it is inaccurate to the point of dishonesty to (mis-)use a sacramental symbol in a manner inconsistent with its finality, its purpose. We will have an opportunity to reflect on the importance of this recognition later in this chapter and again in the forthcoming chapter on ethics.

Let's pause for a moment to consider how a symbol communicates the nature of that which is symbolized by the symbol. For example, if I asked my students about the meaning of baptism, they would surely include in their comments that one of the functions of baptism is a cleansing of sin. Water is used in baptism because water is a suitable symbol for the symbolized cleansing, for water is used in (even) ordinary washing. Mud or motor oil would be unsuitable symbols for cleansing, for they bear no natural resemblance to how cleaning actually works. Likewise, bread and wine are suitable symbols for symbolized spiritual nourishment, but broken glass and thumbtacks are not. These observations, as we will see later, will be important for the moral evaluation of certain sexual acts.

While reflecting on the nature of sacramental symbolism, we also have to reflect on the nature of sacramental action. My point here is to show that just as the nature of the sacramental symbol or its communication is not the result of human decision alone, so too sacramental action has an integrity that is not determined by human will alone and ought not to be violated by human will. Permit me to tell a story to illustrate this point.

When I was a deacon, I was asked to baptize the son of two friends. I found that the parish church did not have a suitable cup or pitcher to pour the water for the sacramental action of the baptismal ritual. Nonetheless, I was able to enact the ritual in a manner consistent with the demands of integral symbolic communication and nature. I immersed my hands into the water of the baptismal font, scooped up some water, and released it over the head of the infant. When I did so, the congregation was able to see and hear the pouring of the water that symbolized the cleansing effects of the baptism itself. While pouring the water, I spoke the prescribed words of the ritual: "I baptize you in the name of the Father ..." I reached into the font a second time, scooped up the water, and while pouring it out, continued with the prescribed words of the ritual: "and of the Son ..." As I did so, the baby's mother moved the boy just a bit, so that instead of the water landing only on his head, the water landed partly on his face, with predictable results. We had to stop for a moment to calm the distressed mother, baby, and deacon, pat the baby on the back, and dry his face.

The rest of the congregation looked on in dismay. I did not feel like continuing with the ritual, as the continuation included the risk that the baby might be moved again and then take another dumping of water in the face, with the consequent consternation of mother, baby, and deacon yet again. In the telling of the story, I would ask my students: "Could I just shrug my shoulders and say, 'Two out of three isn't bad; let's call it a day and just go home!'?" The students insisted that I could not. They knew that the ritual had an integrity of action and formula that must be respected in order for the baptismal action to *effect* a baptism. They knew that I would have to pour out water upon the baby a third time and say, "... and of the Holy Spirit." They would insist that I did not have the authority to change actions and formula that make present and effective that which the baptismal actions, matter, and formula symbolized. I had an obligation to do what the symbolized demanded. It was not up to me to do otherwise. This aspect of sacramental symbolism, we will see later, has significant import for the process of moral evaluation.

We would do well here to pause for a moment and reflect on the notion of authority. The etymology of that word can give us some guidance for understanding moral prescriptions and prohibitions. The word "authority" is drawn from the Latin words *auctor* and *augere*. The former gives us the word "author"; in a moral context, we can then derive words such as "authorize", "authentic", etc. *Augere* gives us the word "augment", meaning to "increase" or to "build up". Taken together, authority is derived from the author of the moral law, which the author gives in order to build up the human community. Just as the elements of sacramental ritual and the proper use of sacramental symbols are set by the proper authority (and not by the whim or will of the sacramental agent), so too human nature and the consequent moral law are set by the author of human nature and not by the whim or will of any moral agent. We will discuss these matters in more detail in the forthcoming chapter on ethics. If we were still in the chapter on metaphysics, I would say that the author of human nature is the Exnihilator, which is consistent with the world view of theism.

Let's review the dynamics of sacramental symbols in action and then apply what we have seen to human sexuality. The sacramental symbol is a mediator, located on the permeable boundary between the public and private dimensions. There is continuity between the symbolized and the symbol taken up in sacramental action. Consequently, the symbol may be understood as an attenuated expression of the symbolized. The human body may function as an announcement of and an invitation toward communion with the person who is privately sustaining and living the publicly available body. With such an understanding in mind, let's have a look at the diagram below, which depicts the human sexual encounter in terms of the symbol taken up in sacramental action.

Sacramental Depiction of Human Mutuality

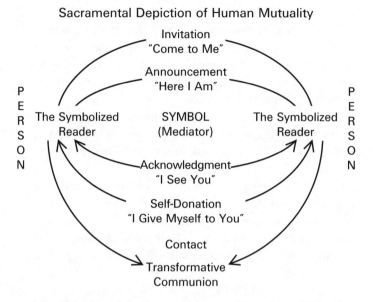

Note that in the diagram above, there is a distinctive emphasis on mutuality. Two persons and their bodies are involved. There must be dual announcements and invitations, with corresponding dual acknowledgment and self-donation, leading to a mutual transformative communion. The scope of this metaphysical and anthropological drama, along with the depth of its moral significance, can be seen if we link our understanding of the sacramentality of the sexual encounter with the Funnel Concept of the Body that we considered earlier along with the notion of truth as an unveiling.

The body unveiled is a sacramental enacting of the revelation of the person privately sustaining and living the body. Just as nakedness affords access to the whole body, so too the sexual encounter, understood sacramentally, affords access to the whole person. The naked body announces the presence of the person; likewise, the naked

body both offers and invites self-donation. The naked
bodies in sexual embrace publicly depict the unseen yet
nonetheless real pouring out of self and the accepting of
the other person. The bodies depict and enact the complete exchange of persons. Herein lies the potential for
human triumph and tragedy.

When enacted according to the moral law inscribed
in human flesh and the human privacy, human bodies in
sexual embrace reveal and tell a deep truth about the
intentions and investments of two persons. It is a most
concrete, public expression of the invisible, privately sustained I-Thou relationship. The public bodies are saying
what the human privacies are meaning. The naked and
united bodies are sacramental symbols of complete self-
donation with the corresponding complete acceptance of
the other self.

It will be useful to recall here two realities. The first
is the hierarchical and reciprocal relations between the
public and private dimensions of the person as depicted
by the Funnel Concept of the Body. The second is the
statement made earlier in this chapter, "I am always more
than just my body, but my body is where you can begin
to find me." Taken together, we can begin to understand
the depths of personal contact symbolically represented
by naked bodies in the sexual embrace. This embrace
represents an I-Thou relationship at the most profound
depth—a giving and receiving of what is most singular,
most unique, of the persons involved. The mystery of
the person, that is, the inexhaustible richness and hidden
depths of the person, is expressed. So understood, we
can understand why cultures of all times and places have
placed rules, laws, customs, rituals, and taboos in the service of protecting human sexuality. Alas, as the Romans
have taught us, *Corruptio optimi pessima est* (the corruption

of the best is the worst). The sexual embrace, which is, as we have said before, a comprehensively human encounter, can go wrong in many ways.

We have made great efforts here to show the complexity of the human person. If the sexual embrace is a comprehensively human matter, then the human sexual encounter can be corrupted and corrupting if any element or aspect of human nature is missing, rejected, or betrayed. Recall that we noted that the sacred is to be unveiled—revealed—only under precisely prescribed circumstances. If the sacred is unveiled in any other way, it is merely exposed and, thus, profaned. So understood, we can see the importance of *consent* in the human sexual encounter. The revelation of the body and the disclosure of the person must be a *self*-disclosure, one undertaken with full (and therefore free) consent. A sexual encounter without consent is a profound and comprehensive act of violence against the whole human person. Because of the nature of the human person and the nature of what the sexual embrace symbolizes, consent is an indispensable element of human sexuality. To do otherwise is to reduce the sexual encounter to the level of I-It; in other words, the encounter treats the person as a mere object rather than as a unique subject. In this context, the body is treated as a non-personified thing, and the person is treated as a non-person.

Thomas Howard, in his brief but very rich work *Chance or the Dance? A Critique of Modern Secularism*, uses sacramental symbolism to depict vividly the anti-human horror and sacrilege of human sexuality enacted contrary to its nature. I will quote him at length here and then comment on his observations:

Promiscuity, either homosexual or heterosexual, is another form of failure to discern the other authentically, for it focuses on the body not as image but as object alone. The sailor who desperately needs something during his overnight in port, the junior executive with his list of telephone numbers in the convention city, the college boy cruising the beach, the old queen in the bar—none of these people feels malicious or even evil. Each has an appetite, there is a perfectly simple way to assuage that appetite, so *en avant*. But the ritual which they seek is a parody. It is like a Black Mass. For both involve all the equipment, movement, and pantomime of the real thing, and both promise a reward indistinguishable at the moment from the reward of the real thing (orgasm; supernatural food). But they are not addressed to the object which the ritual was designed to address. In the Mass, man addresses God and he addresses man, and there is a communion under the species of bread and wine; in sexual intercourse we address the other and the other addresses us, and there is a communion under the species of human anatomy. In the case of bread and wine, of course, it is possible and permissible to throw it away from a picnic table; but the minute you have set it about with a particular intention and ritual it is transformed, and you may no longer throw it away. By the same token, the human body is available for any number of activities (sports, medical inspection, work), but when it is taken into the service of the sexual rite, a universe of significance comes upon it, like God into the Mass, and immediately the participants are less than the thing in which they are participating and it is theirs to observe the rubric with awe. The equipment is no longer merely object; it is image. Taken into the rite, it is transformed. As in poetry, courtesy, ceremony, or any of the ritual ways in which we shape our experience, so here the imposing of a form upon mere function paradoxically elicits the true significance of that function from the raw material. So, for the sailor, the businessman, the boy, and the old queen, another human body is by far the best means of getting a certain kind of pleasure. But it also happens that the human body is the epiphany of personhood. It cloaks and reveals a human individual. A doctor may probe it strictly as a complex of organs and tissue; a gymnastics coach may manipulate it as a pattern of muscles. But the sexual exploration of this mass of tissue and muscle puts the bread and wine on the altar: the real presence of the person must now be reckoned with. The sailor sweating over the strumpet's body is like a priest rushing into the tabernacle and gobbling the bread for a snack. The executive with his call girl, the boy with his trick, the queen with his hustler all participate in the Black Mass which divides form and substance, for it takes the form (the body) and discards the substance (the person); it takes the form (the rite of two bodies) and discards the substance (the union of two persons).[18]

Making use of the sacramental symbolism we have been developing here, Howard summarizes in a concise and vivid way that the perversion of human sexuality is anti-human, depersonalizing, and a sacrilege. Human nature, human bodies, and human sexuality require a respect and reverence that a thoroughly secular world view would be unable to account for, much less facilitate. The sacramental, I-Thou encounter of the sexual embrace is either secured with reverence or destroyed with irreverence. Sexual encounters not in harmony with what the human body means and represents are unworthy of the human persons who live and sustain their sexual bodies.

Howard makes clear that promiscuity is a depersonalizing lie and a sacrilege. To enact an I-Thou encounter through the sexual embrace while treating the body of another person as a merely usable, disposable, and forgettable object is anti-human. What the body means and

[18] Thomas Howard, *Chance or the Dance? A Critique of Modern Secularism* (San Francisco: Ignatius Press, 1989), pp. 124–26.

what the sexual embrace symbolically represents—a total self-giving and simultaneous acceptance of the other self—require a unique, which is say, faithful and exclusive relationship. Neither the broad randomness of indiscriminate promiscuity nor the intermittent use (and thus misuse and abuse) of persons through serial monogamy ("You're my one and only—for now!") is worthy of human nature. Let's take a look at two more highly controversial topics, namely, contraception and homosexuality. We shall look at each topic briefly, not so much in terms of a moral evaluation but rather from the viewpoint of anthropological symbolism.

We have observed that symbolically, the sexual embrace depicts the physical expression of a privately grounded and sustained reality, namely, the complete donation of self and the complete reception of the other self. For the donation and reception to be truly complete, the giving and receiving must include one's fertility. It is simply dishonest to say in the giving of the gift of one's naked body, "I give all of myself to you" while privately stipulating, "Except for my fertility!" Likewise, it is dishonest to say, while receiving the gift of another's naked body, "I accept all of you" while privately stipulating, "Except for your fertility!"

Recall that we observed earlier that there must be a natural resemblance between the symbol and what it symbolizes in order for the symbol to communicate credibly, effectively, and honestly. Water can be used as a symbol of spiritual cleansing, and mud cannot; bread and wine can be used as a symbol of spiritual nourishment, and broken glass cannot. Contracepted sex is an inadequate and dishonest attempt to symbolize what the sexual embrace by its very nature means—total self-donation and total acceptance of the other person. To shout with one's body, "ALL!" while muttering with one's contraception, "But not really ..." is a blameworthy prevarication.

Let's pause for a moment to address three objections to what has been stated above. (1) Is a couple required to intend the procreation of a child with every act of sexual intercourse? (2) What about couples who are infertile or who marry past years of childbearing? (3) What about homosexual acts?

To the first objection: No, one is not required to intend the procreation of a child with every act of sexual intercourse. It should be obvious, however, that one ought to act in a manner consistent with the nature of the symbols and actions that one uses. To symbolize *total* self-donation and *total* acceptance of the gift of another through the entwining of the naked bodies in sexual embrace while deliberately withholding one's fertility and spurning the fertility of another is just dishonest. Contracepted sex is simply a counter-symbol that is contrary to the inherent symbolism of human sexual intercourse. Are there circumstances in which it is morally licit for a couple, open to the transmission of life yet wishing to regulate one's fertility, to use natural means such as "fertility awareness methods" or "natural family planning"? Yes, but to address that topic in any detail would take us too far afield from our present topic.[19]

To the second objection: Regarding the evaluation of the symbolic import of sexual intercourse between an infertile couple, it must be insisted that there is no fault on the part of the couple. The integrity of the act of complete self-donation and complete acceptance of the other's gift

---

[19] Worth examining: Jay Boyd, *Natural Family Planning* (Scotts Valley, Calif.: CreateSpace Independent Publishing Platform, 2013), and Michael Malone, *The Case concerning Catholic Contraception* (Scotts Valley, Calif.: CreateSpace Independent Publishing Platform, 2014).

is intact; nothing is being withheld. The dynamics of the symbolism of intercourse is respected on two levels. First, the complete mutuality symbolized by sexual intercourse is maintained, inasmuch as nothing is being withheld from the act. Second, the symbolism of the male-female complementarity remains—the transmission of the life-giving seed from the male to the seed-receiving chamber of the female is still represented in the act of intercourse even in an infertile couple.

To the third objection: The replies to the first two objections provide resources for the evaluation of the symbolic import of homosexual acts. Some might say, "If sexual intercourse between a heterosexual couple incapable of procreating children is licit, then there can be no objection to homosexual acts that are equally incapable of procreating children." A few distinctions will make clear why that assertion is in error. There is a distinction between *infertility* and *non-fertility*, just as there is a distinction between being blind and being non-sighted. A person blind because of defective eyes might not see, but the organs for seeing are still present. A rock also does not see, but it was never meant to—the organs for seeing were never present. A sighted person might be blinded and so lose sight; a rock, although it cannot see, can never be blinded because it never had the organs for seeing. The capacity for sight can never be symbolized by a rock because by its very nature it is non-sighted. Likewise, homosexual acts are not the symbolic equivalent of heterosexual intercourse, because by their very nature, the former are not *in*fertile but *non*-fertile—they cannot mean what heterosexual intercourse symbolically represents. Also, homosexual acts cannot bring about what the human community needs from human sexuality, namely, to beget the next generation conceived in a loving embrace and to provide children with the mutually committed father and mother that only a husband and wife can provide.

The encounter of the male and female in the sexual embrace brings together humans in a kind of completeness. It is obvious that male and female were made for each other. Father John Harvey[20] frequently said that if you think about the male and female person, how their bodies fit together and what happens when they do, it is obvious that there is only one sexual *orientation*, that of male-female. There may be various *attractions*, but the truth about human persons disclosed through the male body and the female body makes clear that there is only one orientation. Consequently, we can say that homosexual acts are misuses of the sacramental vessels and actions of human sexuality. They are counter-signs.

At this point in our anthropological reflections, we are seeing how apparently disparate elements of human nature must and can be reconciled in a composite anthropology. Without a composite anthropology, the fundamental relations (I-It, I-You, I-Thou) and the fundamental functions (responsibility, attributability, accountability), which are indispensable for any moral agency, are impossible. The root condition of possibility for the fundamental relations and functions is the Permeability Principle: "The public and private dimensions of an actuality are permeable." This fact allows for elements of human nature (including the public and private, the bodily and non-bodily) to remain distinct yet also inseparable. That same kind of connection obtains between two other apparently disparate elements of human nature, namely, that of the rational and the nonrational.

---

[20] See the Courage web site (https://couragerc.org/) and his book *Homosexuality and the Catholic Church* (West Chester, Penn.: Ascension Press, 2007).

You may have noticed that I said "*non*rational" and not *ir*rational. The latter is *contrary* to reason; it is anti-rational—a violation of reason's principles. The nonrational, in this context, includes that which is commonly referred to as the "emotional", but emotion is too narrow a word in this context. Recall what we said about the layers of the privacy when discussing the Funnel Concept of the Body. The nonrational includes the "affective" (understood here as appetite-for-value, mood, and temperament). How might we represent the coherence and interaction of the rational and nonrational in the human person? And how might we do so in a way that can account for him functioning as a moral agent?

*

Since ethics is a practical discipline, dependent upon human moral agents, the challenge before us is to bring together the rational, nonrational, and practical elements of human moral action. We need to have these elements distinct, so that we do not fall into any kind of reductionism. We also need to have these elements in relationship, so as to avoid any form of dualism or solipsism. In other words, we need a properly accurate and adequate account of human action, one that is always holding in composition the various human elements while also maintaining their distinction. We can offer such an account through the various Conjoint Disjuncts.

Conjoint Disjuncts are ways of conceptualizing elements of a reality that are always distinct (thus, disjunctive) while at the same time are also always in relationship (thus, conjunctive). We will look at four Conjoint Disjuncts: the Universal, the Holistic, the Anthropic, and the Fundamental.

The Universal Conjoint Disjunct is so named because it depicts a dynamic of distinction in unity that obtains in every Conjoint Disjunct. We can depict the Universal Conjoint Disjunct with equilateral triangle ABC:

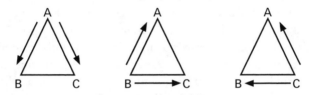

From the viewpoint of A, A is not B; A is not C; A is always in relationship with B; A is always in relationship with C. From the viewpoint of B, B is not A; B is not C; B is always in relationship with A; B is always in relationship with C. From the viewpoint of C, C is not A; C is not B; C is always in relationship with A; C is always in relationship with B. With this dynamic in mind, we can ask, "How do we account for distinctively human action?"

We can do so by making use of the Anthropic Conjoint Disjunct, which depicts the human person as sacramental, as integral, and as relational.

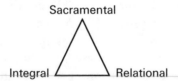

To be the responsible source of one's actions (that is, to be able to say rightly, "I did it") requires that one be sacramental. In other words, the source of privately initiated action lives and sustains a publicly available body in order to express the self through action. The body is the sacramental symbol/vessel of the symbolized human privacy. The momentum of such action is outward, from the private to the public. The necessary antecedent for such an account is a properly transcendent metaphysics, as we saw in the previous chapter. Without a metaphysics that allows for nonmaterial reality, the sacramental dynamism (i.e., the invisible made visible through the physical) is not possible.

Your response to my privately initiated, public action requires that I be integral. You must be able to find me so as to be able to attribute to me my actions as their responsible source ("You did it"). The momentum of such action is inward, from the public to the private. The necessary antecedent for such an account is a composite anthropology.

My morally significant actions indicate that we do not exist in isolation from each other but, rather, that we exist in relationships of various kinds and depths—thus, we must speak of the human person as relational. I may treat another in terms of I-It (or use a person as an object, which is unjust), I-You (treating the person as a subject, which is just), or I-Thou (treating the person in his uniqueness, which is the basis of love). Because we are in relation, you may hold me accountable for the actions you attribute to me as their responsible source. Accountability asks of me as the agent, "Why did you do it?" Depending on my answer, you may then assign me praise or blame. The momentum of accountability is bi-directional, moving back and forth from one person to the next ("Why did you do it?"; "I did it because ..."; "I praise/blame you for your action ..."). The necessary antecedent account of such an account is a sound ethics, expressed via a moral methodology of sufficient explanatory power.

We can now graft the specifically human character of the Anthropic Conjoint Disjunct onto a depiction of the relations among the layers of the Ethical Wedding Cake as a Conjoint Disjunct. This "hybrid" can be depicted as the Holistic Conjoint Disjunct:

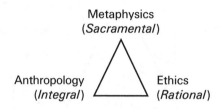

Metaphysics
(*Sacramental*)

Anthropology
(*Integral*)

Ethics
(*Rational*)

When my students see this diagram for the first time, they take it as an illustration of my saying, "Pull on the thread, and you get the whole rug." Sometimes, it may be methodologically convenient to contemplate various themes and considerations separately, but one must be mindful that any account of ethics brings with it a corresponding anthropology and metaphysics. When we hold in proper tension the various elements (by which I mean that we neither reduce one element to any other nor separate them even as we distinguish them), we can account for human moral agency that both does justice to anthropology and points to a sound moral methodology. We are in a position to do so now with a consideration of the Fundamental Conjoint Disjunct.

The Fundamental Conjoint Disjunct is so named because the dynamic depicted there is present in all human moral action. The three elements of this Conjoint Disjunct are reason/logic, affect/imagination, and praxis. Let's look at each element in turn.

Reason/logic describes two different functions of the intellect—they are the rational contribution to moral decision making. The former describes the intuitive/inductive function of the intellect; the latter describes the discursive/deductive function of the intellect. Reason/logic contributes

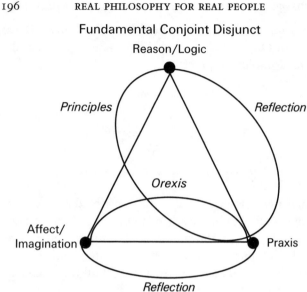

Fundamental Conjoint Disjunct

the principles necessary for ethics as a science. Granted, the principles might be sound (e.g., "Do good and avoid evil") or unsound ("Me always first!"), but principles of some sort are at work in moral decision making. In light of moral principles, moral values may be identified and moral evaluations may be made.

Affect/imagination represents the nonrational contribution to moral decision making. We can better understand the nonrational contribution by reflecting on certain elements of the word "orexis", here understood as the affective and conative character of mental activity as contrasted with its cognitive aspect; the appetitive aspect of an act (in Latin, suggesting longing, appetite; in Greek, to desire).

They contribute the desires and creativity that make ethics an art. Recall that our understanding of affect includes three dimensions. The first is affect as appetite-for-value, that is, the simple inclination toward what is valued—even a very young child can grasp that you should not harm an infant, even if the child cannot explain why. Affect is also understood as both mood and temperament, which can influence how freely one acts in accordance with one's principles, values, and appetite-for-value (about which more later, in the next chapter). Imagination in the Fundamental Conjoint Disjunct serves two functions—empathy and moral creativity. Empathy allows one to place oneself in another's shoes, so to speak. Good parents work hard to train their young children in empathy: "How do you think your sister felt when you took her cookie? How would you feel if she did that to you?" Moral creativity is in evidence when a moral agent applies his principles and values in unfamiliar or unexpected contexts.

Praxis represents the practical dimension of moral reflection. Ethics, after all, is not a speculative discipline. Eventually, a moral agent has to consent to *do* or *not-do* something. Moral praxis is driven by the uniting of principles (the contribution of reason/logic) with appetite-for-value expressed by consent (the contribution of affect/imagination or the orectic power) into a result of morally significant action. A morally mature person, once a moral action is completed, will reflect on his actions. He will ask himself, "How shall I evaluate my action in light of my principles and values? Is my appetite-for-value strong enough to move me to moral action? Did I consent to or withhold consent from a good or evil act? Is the completed action consonant with my principles and my appetite-for-value?"

Before we move on to the next chapter, which is about ethics, let's summarize what a sound (that is to say, composite) anthropology informs us about ethics, especially in light of our understanding of the relevant Conjoint Disjuncts. The nature of the morally good is intimately connected with the nature of the human person. If ethics is an expression of the striving of humanizing and humane perfection, then that standard must be in harmony with what we know about human nature.

We know that the human person is a complex, multi-dimensional actuality, with elements and aspects that are only apparently at odds but that must and can be reconciled. The human person is a unique individual who is always social; he is to be found in the public and private dimensions; he is bodily and non-bodily; rational and non-rational. What could moral behavior of such a complex being look like? What would a sound anthropology enable and demand of an ethics? With these questions, we turn to the Moral Equation (which we will discuss at length in the next chapter about ethics).

Moral Equation

$$RV^2 \rightarrow RD^2 \rightarrow RM \rightarrow RE \overset{UD}{\wedge}$$

where R = right/rightly (rational); D = desire (nonrational); M = means (practical); E = ends (practical); UD = ultimate destiny (metaphysical/transcendent)

Rightly value what is rightly valuable so as to desire rightly what is rightly desirable, giving consent so as to choose the right means to the right ends and thus achieve one's ultimate destiny (*telos*).

The Moral Equation is a linear expression of the Fundamental Conjoint Disjunct. It represents the interactive contributions of every point of the triangle. The elements are not reducible to one another, and so they are disjunctive; they are not separable from one another, and so they are conjoint. The Moral Equation depicts a moral process that leaves out no significant element of the human person. Indeed, it shows that a proper understanding of human moral agency must bring together the various elements and dimensions that were described as "antinomies" in the parable at the outset of this work.

Now that we have a clear sense of what a sound philosophical anthropology offers and requires, let's turn to an extended reflection on ethics in the next chapter.

CHAPTER 6

ETHICS: THE ART AND SCIENCE OF EVALUATING HUMAN BEHAVIOR IN TERMS OF OUGHT AND OUGHT NOT

Art, like morality, consists of drawing the line somewhere.

—G. K. Chesterton

Paul Weiss told me, "One of the most important tests a philosophy can face is what that philosophy allows you to do to other human beings." Rightly understood, Weiss is saying that a critical test of a philosophy is a moral test. A practical philosophy must be livable; it must be, as the title of this book indicates, "Real Philosophy for Real People". A sound, practical philosophy must explain, account for, facilitate, and demand human flourishing— the fulfillment of individuals and communities, both in their uniqueness and in their common human nature. Such is the task of ethics. A coherent and livable ethics must be grounded upon a sound anthropology. Absent a clear account of what a human person is, there can be no hope of identifying human flourishing (such flourishing is the goal of ethics) or of identifying the means toward that end. Likewise, an anthropology cannot stand unless it is built upon a thorough account of the real—in terms of both reality's elements and its temporal horizons—and that is the goal of a sound metaphysics. Absent the foundation that only a thorough and coherent metaphysics can provide, an account of ethics can only be a collection of mere assertions and surmises inferred from hollow or partial premises. Metaphysics and anthropology provide the fixed compass points by which ethics must navigate; real individuals and communities must make the actual trek toward human fulfillment.

We might think of this chapter as the most practical of the book—the chapter you turn to first when you hear a moral claim that seems dubious. Here is what I have in mind: If you were a birdwatcher, you might have a guide book from, say, the Audubon Society. You might observe a bird that is unfamiliar to you. You note its characteristics, plumage, etc., and find a photo of the bird in your guide book. With an "Aha!" of recognition, you confirm the species of the bird you have observed and read more to learn of its habitat, habits, preferred food, etc. Analogously, when you hear a doubtful moral claim and explanation, you can turn to this chapter and, with an "Aha!" of recognition, say, "Oh! This is an instance of moral relativism—and here are its inherent flaws, along with the corresponding antidote." Working back through this book, you can identify the underlying anthropology, along with the corresponding metaphysics, and the world view most congenial to this flawed moral methodology. Having identified the erroneous moral theory, you can apply both refutation and remedy.

The tools of this chapter will allow you to perform the functions of diagnosis, evaluation, and prescription. It can help you to identify those moral methodologies that are various dead ends and can help you to identify and employ a moral methodology that will help you (and the human community) fulfill your (and our) human nature. Let's move on to a brief account of the necessity and benefits of identifying and articulating clearly a moral methodology—which may be understood as a description of the procedures of moral evaluation. From there, we can develop a taxonomy of moral methodologies. Finally, we will identify the best moral methodology, an account of ethics that does justice to the requirements of sound anthropology, metaphysics, and world view.

As we noted before, ethics is a practical discipline. It is an art—a venture that calls for creativity, imagination, and adaptability. It is also a science—a systematic body of knowledge validly derived from identifiable and testable principles. Because there is a human nature and not a mere human happenstance, the moral life of individuals and communities must have access to guidance that is scientific in its structure (as we have described it in this book). At the same time, because the moral life of individuals and communities takes place across a great span of time and in a variety of circumstances and cultural contexts and in our world of rapid change, we must have a way of proceeding that can adapt and thereby meet unexpected challenges and opportunities. The identification of sound and enduring principles, as well as the cultivation of habits of mind and heart, taken together, can help us find the fixed compass points we need in order to navigate well the demands of the moral life in whatever time and place we happen to find ourselves. The goods of this identification and cultivation do not and cannot happen by accident. We need to reflect on our human nature, our individual and collective human experience, and learn from the wisdom and errors of those who have gone before us. So understood, we can understand the need for identifying a sound moral methodology. We cannot, need not, and must not "reinvent the (moral) wheel" with each moment, choice, and act. Absent a reliable moral methodology, we will act impulsively, especially under stress or under the influence of strong appetites. Also, absent a reliable moral methodology, it will be extremely difficult to plan well for our individual and communal lives, cultivate moral character, consistently marshal right means to worthy ends, or raise our children to be healthy and moral.

Before we tackle the various moral methodologies, let's step back and ask ourselves, "What does an ethical system do?" We stated previously that ethics is "the art and science of evaluating human behavior in terms of ought and ought not". What does that evaluation include? Moral evaluation includes discourse about what are known as the three moral determinants: the moral quality of the act itself; the intention of the moral agent; the circumstances in which the act takes place.

One way to distinguish (and ultimately evaluate) various methodologies is to ask, "How does this methodology handle the three moral determinants?" No moral methodology may ignore any one of the three moral determinants. Why?

The *act* is indispensable, because ethics is a practical, not a speculative discipline. The act can be modified by the intention or the situation, but the act is primary. The *intention* too is indispensable, for it is through intention that the agent is the morally responsible source of the act. The *situation and circumstances* are also indispensable, because moral action does not take place in a vacuum.

Some moral methodologies emphasize intention. On this view, primacy is accorded to the will of the agent: Did the agent intend rightly? Some moral methodologies emphasize situation/circumstances: Did the agent act as the situation/circumstances required? Other moral

methodologies see the act itself as the primary moral determinant because actions have qualities in relation to human
nature, needs, and purposes: Did the moral agent act to
link the proper means to achieve the right ends? How
moral methodologies include and rank the three moral
determinants will help us to evaluate each methodology.

Let's turn now to a consideration of the various moral
methodologies that are available to us. What we offer
here is by no means a comprehensive account of every
approach to morals. Ours is a more modest task. We will
examine those schools of moral thought that are most
prevalent today and attend in particular to those that the
ordinary person may encounter in his everyday life. Theories that are particularly obscure or technical or pertain
primarily to a specialized field (e.g., medicine, law, business) are not our primary concern here. We will instead
be treating approaches to ethics that pertain to people of
ordinary intelligence and experience, who are seeking livable answers to practical moral questions. We will not be
addressing specifically the academic or the specialist.

Moral methodologies may be divided into two basic
types, namely, the deontological and the teleological.
Deontological methodologies attend to morality primarily as duty. These methodologies consistently ask: "Am I
doing my duty? Am I obeying the will of the lawgiver?"
And who is "the lawgiver"? We will see shortly that
deontological methodologies are divided according to the
answer to that question.

Teleological (from the Greek *telos*, meaning goal or
end) methodologies attend to morality primarily in terms
of means and ends: "Am I acting for the right end? Am I
using a proper means to a worthy end?" And what is "the
right end"? May I discern the right end according to a rule,
or must each moral evaluation be treated as unique, that is,

on a case-by-case basis? We will see shortly that teleological methodologies are divided according to the answers to those questions.

We can further divide deontological methodologies by looking at the etymology of "deontological". The word is derived from the Greek *deont*—that which is binding (stem of *déon*, neuter present participle of *deîn*, to bind). Most deontological methodologies insist that morality binds us to follow the will of the lawgiver. Is the individual himself the lawgiver, or is the lawgiver someone (or something) other than the moral agent? The various options will be the basis for the various divisions between deontological moral methodologies. What we will see below is that the structural weaknesses inherent in moral methodologies based upon the duty to follow the will of the lawgiver (of whatever kind) will lead to the moral methodology of emotivism, which holds that the moral agent is to be guided by the demands of his emotions. The diagram below may clarify the task ahead of us in this chapter.

Let's look first at morality in terms of the duty to obey the will of the lawgiver, rather than of the nature and needs of the human person. The will of the lawgiver is something imposed either externally or internally. If moral obligation is imposed upon us from outside of ourselves, the lawgiver is either above us (God) or our fellowman. If the morality is considered only in terms of our duty to obey the will of God, we will have the moral methodology known as religious legalism.

The case I want to make here is one that is based upon the Intersecting Model of the relationship between faith and reason that we saw earlier in this book. I will also insist that we need not exclude reference to the divine in philosophical moral discourse—indeed, we must not do so:

Moral Methodologies

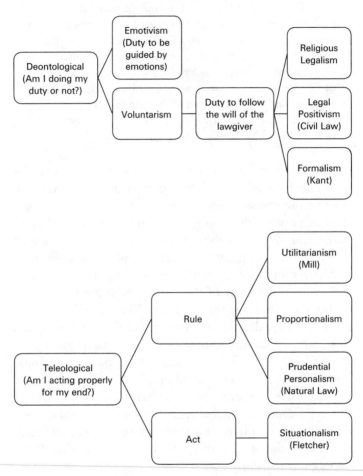

Man is both a physical and a moral being. On his physical side man is governed by physical law in the same way as the other objects that make up the visible creation. But on his moral side, by his knowledge of the moral law and his freedom in applying it to his human acts, man becomes

partaker in his own governance. He is allowed to coop-
erate freely with God in achieving the plan of creation;
without irreverence we may say that he becomes in a fine
and very subordinate manner God's partner. Hence man's
share or participation in the eternal law is much larger than
nonrational creatures can have.... The classical definition
of the natural law ... as identified with the moral law, has
been given by St. Thomas: "The natural law is nothing
else than the rational creature's participation in the eternal
law." (*Summa Theologica*, I-II, q. 91, a. 2.)[1]

Said another way: A persistent curiosity regarding the
antecedents of ethics will lead one to the world view of
theism, the transcendent/Open System metaphysics, and
the composite anthropology that can be the only coherent
foundation for a nonarbitrary ethics, that is, an account of
morality that is rightly prescriptive and not merely hor-
tatory; a moral system that is founded upon the genuine
authority of the giver of the moral law and not the mere
(temporal) power of the lawgiver. The Ethical Wedding
Cake, as I have described it throughout this work, supports
this claim, without requiring a specific act of religious faith
and without moving the discussion from the realm of philosophy to the realm of sacred theology.

Nonetheless, there are those who maintain that no
moral guidance is possible apart from express divine man-
date accessible only to those who have the requisite faith
to receive the special revelation. Such a position I call
"Religious Legalism".

My critique of Religious Legalism is threefold: (1) As a
deontological methodology, it places undue emphasis on
the respective wills of the agent and the lawgiver; (2) It

---

[1] Austin Fagothey, S.J., *Right and Reason*, 2nd ed. (Charlotte, N.C.: TAN
Books, 2009), pp. 172–73.

runs afoul of the conundrum raised by Plato's Socrates in the dialogue known as *Euthyphro*: "Do the gods love something because it is good, or is something good because the gods love it?"; (3) As a methodology, it lends itself to the fideism critiqued earlier in this work.

Regarding the first critique: Religious Legalism, like all deontological methodologies, gives primacy to the moral determinant of intention: What does the moral lawgiver intend? Does the moral agent have a good will (demonstrated by doing his duty to obey the lawgiver) or an evil will (by failing or refusing to do his duty to obey the lawgiver)? Ignoring any reference to context, circumstances, or situation, deontological methodologies fail to do justice to ethics as a practical discipline. All moral acts of human agents occur in time and space and in the context of human relations. Consequently, all human moral acts are *situated*, that is, found in a particular context, located within a nest of circumstances. A deontological methodology makes every moral matter either absolutely "black" or "white", that is, every moral matter is either "evil-because-forbidden" or "good-because-required". There is no legitimate moral gray, points about which honorable men may disagree, as an act may take on a different moral "hue" if it is located in one set of circumstances rather than another. On this view, ethics is always and only a science and never in any way an art.

Perhaps an example will help. Imagine that the lawgiver commands: "All moral agents must follow a healthy diet." What is a "healthy diet"? We can agree that a healthy diet for a twenty-one-year-old male powerlifter will be very different from a healthy diet for a fourteen-year-old female gymnast. It cannot be the case that "one-size-fits-all" applies to the command to follow a healthy diet. Real people, exercising ordinary common sense, can understand

and account for that fact; deontological moral methodologies cannot.

Religious legalism, like all deontological methodologies, ultimately fails because there is no nonarbitrary basis for moral commands or prohibitions. Deontological methodologies are analogous to the parental pronouncement: "Because I said so!" Without a reference to human nature and fulfillment, actions cannot be judged to have intrinsic moral qualities or qualities that can be modified by intention or situation. Morality is an imposed straitjacket rather than an articulation of what human fulfillment is and requires.

Regarding the second critique, the conundrum presented in the Platonic dialogue *Euthyphro*: this critique is related to the first and results from making the intention of the lawgiver the primary moral determinant. In this dialogue, Socrates asks, "Do the gods love something because it is good, or is something good because the gods love it?" According to Socrates, there is no satisfactory answer. If the gods love something because it is good, then the will of the gods is subordinated to that which is good; but such subordination is inconsistent with divinity. If something is good because the gods love it, then ethics is an expression of (admittedly divinely willed) relativism. In other words, there is nothing about murder that is good or evil; all that matters is whether the gods decide to approve or disapprove of it. An ethics predicated upon (even divine) whim, subject to unpredictable, inexplicable, and unaccountable change, is a flimsy basis for the formation of one's character (or the character of one's children) or the formation and continuance of a truly humane community or civilization.

Regarding the third critique of Religious Legalism: Such an approach leads to fideism, which, as noted earlier in this work, undercuts the value of human reason. I recall walking through a church parking lot with a friend, and we happened upon a car with a bumper sticker that read: "GOD SAID IT—I BELIEVE IT—THAT SETTLES IT!" My friend praised the thought (sentiment?) behind the bumper sticker. I was unconvinced: "The bumper sticker tells you nothing about 'God' or what it means for God to have 'said' anything; the bumper sticker tells you nothing about the nature of the person saying 'I' or what is meant by 'I believe'; the bumper sticker uses the word 'IT' three times in apparently three different contexts, without defining or differentiating any of them; the bumper sticker gives no indication of which 'IT' has been 'settled' or what 'SETTLES' means." My friend replied: "And that's why people don't like philosophers!" Such "bumper sticker theology", at once obscure and opaque, cannot be the basis of reasoned moral discourse. Instead, it brings about the Linear Model of Faith and Reason, which disintegrates into caricatures of both faith and reason, as we saw earlier in this book.

What if you wanted to account for ethics using a deontological methodology, but you opted to avoid the complications described above, which are associated with according moral primacy to divine command? Suppose, for example, rather than upon a divine lawgiver, morality were dependent upon a human source—say, the State? In other words, civil government is the source of morality, determining what is good or evil, required or forbidden. Such an approach is called legal positivism. It is called "positivism" because morality is what is *posited*—proposed, asserted, postulated—by the State. In other words, whatever is legal is moral, and whatever is moral is legal.

An illustration may help. I once observed (but had the good sense not to participate in) an online "debate" regarding abortion. One participant wrote: "It doesn't matter whether you like abortion or not. In America, abortion is

LEGAL! Get over it!" In more sophisticated venues, say, the Senate Judiciary Committee hearings interviewing a nominee to the Supreme Court, one might be asked whether or not one accepts *Roe vs. Wade* as "the settled Law of the Land". In other words: "It doesn't matter whether you like abortion or not. In America, abortion is LEGAL! Get over it!"

Such a view might be appealing if one's view is in fact in accord with what is, at present, "the settled Law of the Land". It may be comforting to know that the duty to comply with the Law of the Land is enforced by people with badges and guns when the law meets your approval and supports your interests. Life looks very different, however, when the law is not in your favor, harms your interests, or threatens your life. And on this view, there is no such thing as a bad law, an immoral law, or justification for opposing what is required or forbidden by law. There is only the duty to obey the laws promulgated by the State. But no sane person (or community) could tolerate a moral methodology that might, say, require one to kill one's parents as "useless eaters" or betray one's conscience.

Legal positivism, in brief, suffers from all the fatal flaws inherent in any deontological moral methodology, as described above. In addition, legal positivism is a moral theory with a very bloody past—a past still recent enough to be part of living memory. Legal positivism is the foundation of democide, which is defined by political scientist R.J. Rummel as "the murder of any person or people by their government, including genocide, politicide and mass murder". According to Rummel, the single largest cause of death in the twentieth century is the State killing its own citizens. He puts the body count at 262,000,000.[2]

---

[2] http://www.hawaii.edu/powerkills/20TH.HTM.

Legal positivism can have no objections to these deaths, because, with the State as the agent, these deaths were legal and, therefore, by definition, moral.

If one insisted on maintaining the viability of a deontological moral methodology and yet did not wish to accord the status of "lawgiver" to God or to the State, the only option left would be the autonomous individual as lawgiver. This brings us to the moral philosophy of Immanuel Kant, arguably the most influential theorist advocating the primacy of duty in morality.

Let's consider the etymology of "law". In Greek, the root word of law is *nomos*. Kant rejected "heteronomy", that is, legislation from another, whether that other is God or the State. Instead, he advocated autonomy, that is, self-legislation. Morality consists in imposing duty upon oneself. Each individual is his own lawgiver. In fact, the "dignity of a rational being" depends upon obeying "no law except that which he himself also gives".[3]

How does Kant avoid complete moral relativism—the chaos of each individual as a moral law unto himself? He claims we can avoid such traps by means of "universalizability". On this view, the way to test a proposed course of moral action is to ask whether one would will that the action be required of all:

> There is one imperative which directly commands a certain conduct without making its condition some purpose to be reached by it. This imperative is categorical. It concerns not the material of the action and its intended result but the form and principle from which it results. What is essentially good in it consists in the intention, the result

[3] Immanuel Kant, *Foundations of the Metaphysics of Morals*, trans. Lewis White Beck, 2nd ed. (New York: Macmillan; London: Collier Macmillan, 1990), section II.

being what it may. The imperative may be called the imperative of morality.... There is, therefore, only one categorical imperative. It is: Act only according to that maxim by which you can at the same time will that it should become a universal law.[4]

Kant offers an illustration. Could it be right to make a false promise in order to extricate oneself from some difficulty? He suggests that we ask ourselves, "Would I be content that my maxim (of extricating myself from difficulty by a false promise) should hold as a universal law for myself as well as others?" Kant argues that we must answer in the negative, and so one has the duty not to make a false promise. We will see shortly that this approach, absent moral content apart from motive, will lead to a moral methodology that Kant would find abhorrent—namely, emotivism.

Kant holds that the motive of duty—and duty *alone*—gives actions moral quality. Apart from a universalized categorical imperative, an action has no moral quality, no moral meaning. Is that really livable? Picture this: A married couple goes to dinner to celebrate their twenty-fifth wedding anniversary. The husband rhapsodizes to his wife, thanking her for twenty-five years of faithful, joyful, sacrificial love, through all the ups and downs, across the miles and the years of their marriage. And the wife replies, "No need to thank me! I was just doing my duty!" Surely that would put a damper on the evening, wouldn't it? Are we really fully human if there is no moral significance accorded to love, passion, generosity, self-sacrifice?

Kant would also be at pains to account for heroism, which has been praised in all times and places. Will he

---

[4] Ibid.

deny the goodness of heroes and their moral feats and sacrifices? Or will he say that at all times and everywhere,
all moral agents must be either heroes or moral failures?
A universal requirement of heroism, practically speaking,
would be impossible to bear. And, logically speaking, if
heroism is the moral minimum, it ceases to be heroic.

At root, Kant's morality is hollow. We can see this
more clearly when we consider that his approach to ethics is sometimes known as "formalism" because it gives
the *form* of morality (i.e., duty, the categorical imperative,
universalizability) but it gives no *content*. Kant's morality is
an abstraction, absent consideration of the anthropological
complexity of the human moral agent (as we saw in chapter 5) and offers no consideration of the moral qualities of
actions in relation to human nature, needs, purposes, and
ultimate fulfillment. At most, he offers the logical form
of moral rules but does not supply content. Ironically, in
an attempt to fill in the vacuum left by the abstraction of
Kantian formalism, his sober morality of duty led to the
primacy (and ultimately tyranny) of emotions:

> It is true that he proposed four applications forbidding
> suicide and lying, and commanding the development of
> one's talents and striving to help others, but his argu-
> ments for the first two are dubious and the positive com-
> mandments remain entirely abstract. Hence, after Kant
> but contrary to his view, ethicists found that in order to
> descend from Kant's universal, very abstract principles to
> actual moral decisions in concrete cases they were forced
> again to resort to Romanticism, with its aesthetic con-
> struction of values on the basis of essentially subjective and
> emotional preferences. This became the ethical method-
> ology called emotivism. Each culture or community or
> even each individual constructs a lifestyle based on certain
> emotional attitudes of approval or disapproval, which then

becomes the standard for ethical judgment of what is good or bad behavior.[5]

Unfortunately, as a moral methodology, emotivism, in its various guises, is as faulty as it is popular. In one form, emotivism is the Romantics' overreaction to the desiccated, less-than-human abstraction of Kant's dutiful morality. The Romantics produced some great art, literature, and music and, alas, some highly influential and deeply flawed philosophy. With a dramatic flourish, the Romantics opened the door to the more lazy and thoughtless moralizing that we see today in popular culture. Nowadays, it seems that the prefatory remark "I feel that ..." announces incontestable moral authority.

The differences between the uses of emotivism by Romantics of the eighteenth to nineteenth centuries and the uses of emotivism in contemporary culture are instructive. Among the former, at the root of emotivism was a duty to answer the call of the heart, to embrace one's duty to walk in the illumination that could come only from one's emotions. There was a sense of dignity and grandeur in dutifully heeding the demands of emotion. Emotivism practiced by Romantics had an aesthetic as well as moral quality—a concern for beauty along with goodness.

In contrast, contemporary emotivists, while according primacy to the demands of emotions, tend toward what is base rather than beautiful:

> *You and me, baby ain't nothin' but mammals*
> *So let's do it like they do on the Discovery Channel*[6]

---

[5] Benedict M. Ashley et al., *Health Care Ethics: A Catholic Theological Analysis*, 5th ed. (Washington, D.C.: Georgetown University Press, 2006), p. 11.

[6] Bloodhound Gang, "The Bad Touch Song", MetroLyrics, visited January 27, 2020, http://www.metrolyrics.com/discovery-channel-lyrics-bloodhound -gang.html.

Another significant difference between emotivists past and present is that while the former insisted on bowing to their *own* emotions, contemporary emotivists insist that you bow to *their* emotions. Members of so-called "Generation Snowflake", now of college age, either riot on university campuses when speakers say things that students might find upsetting, or they retire to "safe spaces", replete with soft music, pillows, puppies, and crayons, so that they might be soothed after hearing something they found to be "offensive" or "triggering". Some universities even offer a "Safe Space Glossary" of non-offensive terms, lest anyone's emotions be stirred into unpleasantness.[7] Such dynamics, wittingly or not, quash moral discourse and debate.

Emotivism, whether of the Romantic or "Snowflake" variety, is irredeemably flawed moral methodology. First, it has all the limitations inherent in any deontological methodology, as noted above. In addition, elevating one aspect of human life (emotions) to the exclusion of all else fails to do justice to the multi-dimensional complexity of the composite anthropology that a sound ethics requires.

This overview of the forms of deontological methodologies that the common person is likely to encounter allows us to draw a few conclusions. While duty is an indispensable element of morality, it cannot by itself bear the full weight of ethics. Deontological methodologies depend upon a stunted view of the human person, giving primacy to the will and short shrift to reason and its ability to know human nature and what human flourishing offers and requires. According primacy to the moral determinant of intention is inherently flawed. If we are to have a sound

---

[7] "Glossary of Terms", Old Dominion University, Safe Space, visited January 27, 2020, https://www.odu.edu/safespace/glossary.

ethics, we must, while never forgetting the importance of duty, turn away from deontological methodologies and consider teleological methodologies. And we must consider whether ethics is best grounded upon the primacy of situation/circumstance or upon the primacy of the moral act itself.

> An ends-means methodology in ethics seeks to justify or reject an action, not simply by some accepted code of right and wrong but by determining whether it is an effective or a self-defeating means to the end or goal of true human fulfillment in the community. Some persons choose as their goal in life some kind of illusory self-fulfillment that when it is attained leaves them miserable, such as the man who devotes all his energies to financial success, only to discover that he is rich, lonely, and afraid of death. Yet even when we have chosen the true goal in life, a happiness that is authentic, we still have the right to choose means that will really achieve it and avoid those that promise to achieve it but will ultimately fail.[8]

Teleological methodologies seek to identify worthy ends and to discern and then link the right means to those ends. These methodologies vary in their points of emphasis. They also vary in how (in)adequate their use of anthropology may be. Let's begin with a (deceptively) simple methodology that has been highly influential, that of situationalism, in particular, as it has been expounded by Joseph Fletcher.

The very name indicates that the methodology accords primacy to the moral determinant of the situation/circumstances in which the action takes place. Fletcher's seminal work *Situation Ethics: The New Morality* was first published

---

[8] Ashley et al., *Health Care Ethics*, p. 14.

in 1966. In it he rejected guidance from universal principles, claiming that moral agents are unique and each moral
judgment takes place within a context that can never be
repeated. Each moral decision is incomparable. There is
nothing or no one able to require rightly or forbid absolutely; nothing is intrinsically good or evil. In a sense, each
moral decision represents an act of creation, a coming-
to-be of something unique, emerging from the intersection
of choice and the flux of daily life. So understood, the "old
ethics"—the moral systems that depend upon black-or-
white, duties, obligations, universals—just breaks down.
For Fletcher, moral decision making may be compared to
the account of time as only the "Now" that was described
in chapter 4 of this work. The moral moment, so to speak,
is unrelated to what came before or after it. No moral
guidance or obligation can touch or illuminate this particular, unique moral moment. "Any moral ... judgment ...
is a *decision*—not a conclusion."[9] In other words, a moral
evaluation is not and cannot be derived from principles.
Ethics, on Fletcher's view, can never be a science. But
even when ethics is understood as an art, moral evaluation
cannot be merely random, any more than a great painting
can be only random flecks flung at a bare canvas. Although
he does not expressly reject moral principles absolutely, he
has resolved to keep them on a very short leash: "Situation
ethics keeps principles sternly in their place, in the role of
advisers without veto power!"[10]

He is surely an ethical antinomian—but is that all
that can be said about Fletcher? Might he be described
as an ethical anarchist or nihilist? Fletcher himself would

[9] Joseph Fletcher, *Situation Ethics: The New Morality* (Philadelphia: Westminster John Knox Press, 1966), p. 47.
   [10] Ibid., p. 55.

deny such labels. His claim is that moral judgments may be rightly made based—solely—on love. He cautions us, however, not to expect much from love as the foundation of morality, saying that we cannot "milk universals from a universal".[11] He wants to reject the notion of "unwritten ... laws of heaven".[12] He is at pains, though, to give any content to what he means by "love", without then building up a moral system, when system-building is precisely what he himself rejects. He lauds love: "there are no universals of any kind. Only love is objectively valid, only love is universal.... The situationist holds that whatever is the most loving thing in the situation is the right and good thing. It is not excusably evil, it is positively good."[13] He also insists that love is self-justifying: "Nothing makes a thing good except agapeic expedience; nothing *can* justify an act except a loving purpose."[14]

The most he can do is speak of love as a "normative ideal" that is somehow related to the *agape* of the New Testament, but without requiring any faith commitments.[15] In the foreword to *Situation Ethics* he writes:

> Over the years, as I have lectured on non-Christian systems of ethics, comparing them to various Christian systems, I have sometimes included my own *non*system. It is this "nonsystem" which is set forth in capsule form in these pages. In some cases my critics ... have argued that my point of view actually represents a Christian system of nonethics.... The reader will find a method here, but no system. It is a method of "situational" or "contextual"

[11] Ibid., p. 27.
[12] Ibid., p. 30.
[13] Ibid., pp. 64–65.
[14] Ibid., p. 125.
[15] Ibid., p. 15.

decision-making, but system-building has no part in it....
I am inclined to say that *any* ethical system is unchristian
or at last sub-Christian, whatever might be its claim to
theological orthodoxy.[16]

While eschewing any systematic approach to morality,
Fletcher also insists that we are not left with a moral vacuum: "There are at bottom only three alternative routes
or approaches to follow in making moral decisions. They
are: (1) the legalistic; (2) the antinomian ..., i.e., a law-
less or unprincipled approach; and (3) the situational."[17]
He accords primacy to the situation of the moral act, and
"love"[18] is the sufficient and sole guidance suitable for discerning what action to take in any given situation:

The situationist enters into every decision-making situation fully armed with the ethical maxims of his community and its heritage, and he treats them with respect as
illuminators of his problems. Just the same he is prepared
in any situation to compromise them or set them aside
in the situation if love seems better served by doing so.
Situation ethics goes part of the way with natural law, by
accepting reason as the instrument of moral judgment,
while rejecting the notion that the good is "given" in the
nature of things, objectively. It goes part of the way with
Scriptural law by accepting revelation as the source of the
norm while rejecting all "revealed" norms or laws but
the one command—to love God in the neighbor. The
situationist follows a moral law or violates it according to
love's need.[19]

[16] Ibid., pp. 11–12.
[17] Ibid., p. 17.
[18] "Situation ethics ... calls upon us to keep law in a subservient place, so
that only love and reason count when the chips are down!" Ibid., p. 31.
[19] Ibid., p. 26.

In light of the work we have done throughout this book, the flaws of Fletcher's situationalism should be readily apparent. It gives an undue emphasis to the situation/circumstances in which moral judgments and actions take place. It pays scant attention to anthropology and metaphysics. Absent a clear account of human nature, human needs, and human fulfillment, and lacking an account of divine wisdom expressed in moral absolutes, Fletcher can only extol "love as the only law" but cannot justify it or even adequately describe it. Instead, he clears a path for a kind of sentimentality that leads to moral license.

I summarize my critique of Fletcher to my students this way: "Imagine receiving a proposal of marriage. And before you can answer, your beloved adds, 'Of course, absolute fidelity is a noble ideal—but who believes in absolutes anymore? If I go to work, and I find that my assistant is in distress and needs a special kind of loving that only sex can give, well, in that situation, the loving thing to do may actually be to cancel my appointments and book a hotel room for a zesty session of impromptu consolation!' Would you then accept the marriage proposal?" The students would not stand for it, but Fletcher would have to allow it.

Let's pause for a moment and consider the role that situation/circumstances play in moral evaluation and action. These can color what is required (or forbidden) of a moral agent:

> It is evident that a human act can have its morality colored by the circumstances in which it is done. No act can be done in the abstract; every act actually performed is surrounded by a number of concrete circumstances involving persons, quantity, quality, place, time, manner, means, frequency, and relations of all sorts. These circumstances can be foreseen and willed in the willing of the act. In this

event, they contribute to the morality of the act, either
giving it a new moral species or a new degree within
the species.[20]

A situational morality erroneously accords primacy
to one moral determinant, while underplaying or even
discounting entirely the other moral determinants. Yes,
common sense makes clear that situation/circumstances
are not morally irrelevant. What is needed is a situated
morality, one that can allow for proper acknowledgment of
situation/circumstances, without the other moral determinants being overshadowed or displaced. A situated morality allows ethics to be an art without robbing ethics of its
status as a science. Perhaps an illustration may help.

Let's say you have a nine-year-old son. You know that
if he goes to bed after 8 P.M., he is grumpy the following
morning and does not do well in school that day. So, the
8 P.M. bedtime is a clear and firm requirement of Junior's
daily routine. Now imagine tucking him at 8 when he
says, "By the way, there was a shooting in the playground
at school today. I'm very upset about it and would sure
like to talk about it." Would you really say, "Tut tut!
You know the rule! 8 P.M. is lights out! You should have
thought of bringing this up earlier. It will have to wait till
morning. Good night—pleasant dreams!" Of course not!
A situated morality would allow for the exception to the
rule without dispensing with the rule entirely and without
undercutting the status of moral rules as a whole. Learning
to discern how to read situations and when to allow for
exceptions falls to the virtue of prudence, which we will
discuss later.

Ethics, as we have said, is a practical discipline. Fletcher's
situationalism offers so little guidance as to be impractical.

[20] Fagothey, *Right and Reason*, pp. 150–51.

What if there were a moral methodology that prided itself on its practicality? What if there were a moral methodology that kept its focus squarely on *results* and on linking the most efficient means to desired ends? We turn now to consider the moral methodology of utilitarianism.

Utilitarianism is often associated with two other approaches to ethics, namely, hedonism and consequentialism. Utilitarianism, rightly understood, is an intersection of the two. Hedonism asserts that human motivation may be explained by the pursuit of pleasure and the avoidance of pain. On this view, the moral exhortation to "Do good and avoid evil" is simply a call to act for the sake of the pursuit of pleasure and the avoidance of pain. Hedonism may be understood as existing on a spectrum. Pleasures may range from the most base (e.g., the notorious "sex, drugs, and rock-n-roll" lifestyle) to the most refined. Likewise, the pursuit of pleasure and avoidance of pain may range from the most selfish to the altruistic.

Consequentialism evaluates moral actions in terms of the results that the actions bring about. Having a happy ending is more important than how you got there. The ends justify the means. Means themselves are neither moral nor immoral; they are either effective or ineffective, efficient or inefficient.

Let's bring these two strands, hedonism and consequentialism, and see how they come together in utilitarianism. Utilitarianism is consequentialism for the sake of hedonism. The two foundational figures of utilitarianism, Bentham and Mill, both had a strong sense of the common good, of social conscience. They each argued for an approach to morality that was generous, altruistic, practical, and communal. They understood morality as a plan to bring about the greatest happiness (i.e., maximum pleasure and minimum pain) for the greatest number of people.

Jeremy Bentham is recognized as the grandfather of utilitarianism. He claimed that units of pleasure and pain could be calculated arithmetically, measured in "units of satisfaction". Utilitarians came to speak of a "moral calculus" that would allow one to plan out, in a kind of cost-benefit analysis, the outcomes of gains and losses of pleasures and pains, for the individual and for the human community at large, with considerable precision. One need not strain to imagine how this view might appeal to bureaucrats who, armed with the power of the State and with confidence in their calculations, are certain that they know what is best and that they know how to bring maximum benefit to the many, if not to all.

Such a view can lead to most grievous mischief and worse. It can lead to a limitless tyranny, driven not by ideological dogmas but by an appallingly smug certainty that never rests. C. S. Lewis warned:

> Of all tyrannies, a tyranny sincerely exercised for the good of its victims may be the most oppressive. It may be better to live under robber barons than under omnipotent moral busybodies. The robber baron's cruelty may sometimes sleep, his cupidity may at some point be satiated; but those who torment us for our own good will torment us without end for they do so with the approval of their own conscience. They may be more likely to go to Heaven yet at the same time likelier to make a Hell of earth. This very kindness stings with intolerable insult. To be "cured" against one's will and cured of states which we may not regard as disease is to be put on a level of those who have not yet reached the age of reason or those who never will; to be classed with infants, imbeciles, and domestic animals.[21]

[21] C. S. Lewis, *God in the Dock* (Grand Rapids, Mich.: Eerdmans, 2015), p. 324.

More prosaically, the difficulties of utilitarianism are summarily articulated:

> But how can we find a common quantitative unit of measurement for the qualitatively very different kinds of "satisfactions" that make up a truly fulfilled life? Can I weigh the price of friendship, success in my work, and good health one against another? Can we sacrifice the life of one innocent person to save the lives of ten others? How in medical ethics can we predict whether the patient's future health will give enough pleasure to outweigh the pain of surgery?[22]

Bentham and those like him would have to maintain that pleasures and pains are both comparable and quantifiable—but that just flies in the face of common sense and ordinary human experience. It also rests upon the assumption (one that is easily shown to be unfounded) that the consequences of our actions can be predicted accurately, thoroughly, and consistently. History suggests otherwise. The annals of history are replete with accounts of grand ideas that, once executed, brought about unintended or unforeseen results. Napoleon, when he launched his invasion of Russia, did not expect to return to France with but 10 percent of his troops alive. On a much smaller scale, we can see that claims to predict with accuracy and completeness the outcome of our actions are overstated. I ask my students, "How many times have you planned a course of action, acted, and then found yourself saying, 'Well, I sure didn't see *that* coming!'?" Every hand goes up.

If Bentham is the grandfather of utilitarianism, John Stuart Mill is the father. His approach is more accommodating than that of Bentham. Mill saw that pleasures differ

---

[22] Ashley et al., *Health Care Ethics*, p. 15.

in quality as well as quantity and that there are higher and lower pleasures: "It is better to be a human being dissatisfied than a pig satisfied; better to be Socrates dissatisfied than a fool satisfied."[23] Nonetheless, Mill's approach to morals is subject to the same criticisms that apply to Bentham's approach.

The common flaws of all forms of utilitarianism are fourfold: (1) It is impossible to predict all the consequences of our actions. (2) Some goods/evils are not subject to quantification or comparison. (3) Utilitarianism cannot justify, on its own terms, the altruism that it requires. (4) Wittingly or not, utilitarianism opens some moral doors that must remain closed.

The first critique, that of unpredictability, is easy enough to articulate and understand. Regarding the second, ordinary experience and common sense indicate that some goods cannot be measured. What "price" can be put on a holiday with a beloved grandchild? Who can know with certainty that the pain of chemotherapy is worth enduring for the sake of attending a neighbor's wedding? How can those questions be answered by those who do not have to live through and with the consequences of those decisions?

The greater challenges to utilitarianism come from the third and fourth critiques. This methodology claims to bring about "the greatest good for the greatest number". Let us grant that—for now. What if you are not part of the "greatest number"? What if the increase in social happiness and pleasure is brought about at your expense and pain? How can the hedonistic calculus of utilitarianism *oblige* altruism? How can a *hedonistic* moral methodology require sacrifice?

[23] John Stuart Mill, *Utilitarianism*, 2nd ed. (Indianapolis: Hackett, 2002), chap. 2.

The fourth critique identifies the dark underside of utilitarianism, namely, the precarious status of the human individual. While speaking broadly of the "greatest good for the greatest number", what value does utilitarianism accord to the individual person? Is an individual only a part of a greater whole? Is an individual's value understood only in terms of utility for the collective? What can the hedonism underlying utilitarianism say to individuals who are expected to sacrifice themselves for the "greater good"? Sadly, the twentieth century in particular is full of blood-soaked examples of the individual and the many being sacrificed for the "greater good" of the collective, of the masses. I summarize to my students my critique of utilitarianism this way: "Utilitarianism starts by crunching numbers, and it ends by crunching people." This point can be illustrated by a quote often attributed to Soviet dictator Josef Stalin, arguably the most accomplished mass murderer of the twentieth century: "The death of one man is a tragedy; the death of millions is a statistic." Contemporary utilitarian bureaucrats can quickly become quite comfortable in dealing with statistics—to the detriment of the communities they supposedly serve and to the deaths of millions of individuals, individuals whose unique preciousness the bureaucrats are unwilling to consider and are unable to account for.

We seem to be running out of options for a sound moral methodology. The flaws of deontological methodologies prompted us to turn to teleological methodologies. So far, situationalism and utilitarianism have not measured up. Although these two are very different from one another, they share a common flaw—both place exclusive emphasis on a single indispensable moral component. Each of these methodologies collapsed under the weight placed upon a single point. We agree with the situationalists that situation/circumstances must not be ignored in moral evaluation; we part from them because their according absolute primacy to situation leads to moral anarchy. We agree with the utilitarians that a concern for outcomes should not be ignored; we part from them because their methodology claims too much, ignores too much, and has been used enthusiastically and confidently to justify mass murder for a "greater good". In both cases, the methodologies had a single failure point. What if we could have a methodology that combined a variety of elements in order to allow for the complexity of human decision making, especially in a world of constant change? As we raise this question, the moral methodology of proportionalism steps forward to be considered.

Proportionalism emerged in the 1960s, starting with Catholic theologians.[24] Their claim was that they wanted to avoid the arid legalism of the old theology manuals (which, on their account, were just catalogues of sins and penalties); they wanted to avoid the austerity and sterility of Kantian formalism; they wanted flexibility/adaptability suited for a world of rapid change, but they wanted more guidance than Fletcher's situationalism; they wanted to avoid the strictures, rigidity, and lack of moral imagination imposed by (what they perceived to be) outmoded moral reasoning coming from the methodologies influenced by Aristotle, Saint Thomas Aquinas, and the classical natural law tradition.

The central maxim of proportionalism is: "Do only those acts for which there is a proportionate reason in their favor." Let's take a first look at this methodology in terms of its similarities and differences in relation to other moral methodologies, and then we will begin our evaluation:

---

[24] These would include Joseph Fuchs, Richard McCormick, Bernard Haring, Charles Curran, Peter Knauer, and Bruno Schuller.

[Proportionalists] ... deny they are utilitarians or conse-
quentialists, because they do not simply weigh the good
and bad consequences of an act, but more inclusively
weigh all its "values" and "disvalues." Yet in common
with utilitarianism and consequentialism, proportionalists
reject the traditional view that some kinds of concrete acts
can *never* serve as means to true happiness and hence are
intrinsically evil and are forbidden by absolute (exception-
less) moral norms. They reject such absolute norms because
they maintain that it is always possible to imagine unusual
circumstances in which what would ordinarily be an evil
act can be justified, especially when performed for a good
intention. For example, some proportionalists argue that in
certain circumstances and with good intention contraception and even abortion are morally good, because they are
done with a good intention in order to achieve positive
values that outweigh the disvalues of the act.[25]

Perhaps we can summarize the import of proportionalism more simply. A moral legalist presents all of morality as black or white; there is what is forbidden and what
is required and nothing else. There may be no honorable disagreement. A moral nihilist presents all of morality as undifferentiated gray. On such a view, the maxim
may be: "Do what you can to get what you want, and
let only the strong survive!" Proportionalism rejects completely the black or white of morality—there are no acts
that are always forbidden/evil or always required/good. At
the same time, they wish to avoid the moral nihilism that
reduces the moral sphere to undifferentiated (and morally
insignificant) gray. Instead, they wish to argue for what
might be called "shades of gray". The goal of the moral life
is to end up with (proportionately) more light gray than

[25] Ashley et al., *Health Care Ethics*, pp. 15–16.

dark gray. What constitutes what is lighter gray rather than darker gray? Well ... that is up to you.

According to proportionalism, actions do not have moral qualities—actions are "pre-moral" unless and until you assign values to them. With your own moral calculus, which is updated constantly as your situation/circumstances change, you assign "value" to some facts of your life and "disvalue" to some other facts of your life. Once you assign value/disvalue, you weigh your options and choose the one that has a proportionate reason in its favor, i.e., "Because of the values/disvalues I have assigned to the pre-moral facts of my situation, I choose the option that leads me to proportionately lighter rather than darker gray."

An astute observer might notice that proportionalism combines the weaker features of several moral methodologies. It makes use of the moral calculus of utilitarianism, along with the latter's confidence in predicting moral outcomes; there is the emphasis on the uniqueness of circumstances that is characteristic of situationalism; there is the inability to offer a rational, nonarbitrary account of value and obligation that one expects of emotivism. One might summarize proportionalism as "moral relativism with a Ph.D." It seems better suited for moral rationalization than for moral reasoning. It is a way of calculating how you feel about an action and its expected outcome. While this methodology is confident about predicting outcomes and consequences, it offers little in the way of examining how moral actions affect the formation (or deformation) of character. Proportionalism might offer a rationale for selecting abortion (e.g., "I assign a greater value to finishing my degree on time than to the disvalue of procuring an abortion"), but it offers no resource for pondering how killing your preborn child will affect your character.

"How do I feel about my choice" is different from "What kind of person will my choice make me?" To ask the latter question is to move into an environment of moral realism in which proportionalism cannot long survive.

As I sat here writing this, I was tempted to say that, "The allure of proportionalism is that it allows you to rationalize *any* action while still allowing you to feel good about yourself because in acting as you did, you were true to yourself." But that is not quite right. Proportionalism does not recognize a concrete, essential human nature to which it can be true—or to which it can fail to be true. Once a common, knowable, and fixed human nature is identified, then certain actions are evil and forbidden because they lead to human dissolution or they are good and required because they lead to human flourishing and fulfillment. Once you start thinking like that, then certain actions have natural, intrinsic moral qualities, regardless of intention or situation. Recognizing a human nature to which you could be true or which you could betray puts expectations and limits on moral human action. That would lead us to the way of thinking of classical natural law theory, which is precisely what proportionalism was designed to avoid.

Proportionalism is a methodology of expedience rather than coherence. Moral action, on this view, would be idiosyncratic, evidently flowing from a human happenstance striving to be pleasured and convenienced rather than completed and perfected. At best, it can offer excuses that are intelligible and plausible only for the one making the excuses. Severed from an identifiable, common, and perennial human nature, it cannot offer prescription or prohibition—much less can it produce moral heroes. (Can Frank Sinatra singing "I Did It My Way" really be a moral exemplar?) And how can a moral methodology founded upon an anthropology of human happenstance be truly teleological? After all, there may be goal-seeking, but there is no objective standard or *telos* to reach or fall short of.

It seems that we have nearly run out of options in our search for a sound moral methodology. What we need is a way of moral evaluation that uses fixed compass points of black and white by which we may navigate through options that are legitimately morally gray. We need a moral methodology that does justice to every aspect of the composite anthropology discussed in the previous chapter. This methodology will require the realism of a transcendent/Open System metaphysics. As well, it will require the impetus of *entelechia*—the impetus toward fulfillment, the inner drive toward *telos*—and the terminus of teleology that only the world view of theism can provide.

What we are looking for in one sense might be described as "premodern", because it is a claim to moral realism based on the orientation of human nature toward the divine nature—a stance that the naturalists and those who came after them could scarcely countenance. (Here there comes to mind the memory of my interview for a teaching position when a statement I made caused this outburst from one of my interviewers: "My God! You're a moral realist!" In context, this fact counted against me.)

At the same time, it should be noted that the moral methodology we are looking for should be acknowledged as "postmodern"—on the condition that "postmodern" is rightly understood. In the sense that I mean it here, to call the sought-for moral methodology "postmodern" is to admit that we must not forget all we have learned (and all we may have to unlearn[26]) from the

---

[26] Peter Augustine Lawler's *Postmodernism Rightly Understood: The Return to Realism in American Thought* (Lanham, Md.: Rowman & Littlefield, 1999) is a useful resource for those who would reclaim the word "postmodernism".

centuries that have ensued since the decline of theism, the rise of naturalism/modernism, and the oceans of ink and blood that have flowed from those transitions and their aftermath.

Certainly, anyone with a clear sense of human history since the French Revolution must admit that we can no longer afford to manage our moral life with denatured humans in the foreground and dismissed divinity in the background.

Postmodern, insofar as it has learned from the errors of modernity and its aftermath, the moral methodology we seek will require that we again acknowledge as persons both man and God. With these conditions in mind, we turn now to the moral methodology known as prudential personalism.

Prudential personalism, as a moral methodology, is a statement, in contemporary idiom and context, of the best of the classical natural law tradition of Western civilization, having the benefit of being at once properly pre- and postmodern. Premodern, it rests upon the transcendent realities and common practicalities once acknowledged as foundational for Western civilization. Properly postmodern, it is cognizant of the achievements and calamities of the human experience after the eclipsing of both man and God by materialism after the emergence of naturalism as a predominant world view.

Not merely nostalgic, prudential personalism looks to the past and would retrieve the lessons and realities once considered dispensable since the abandonment of theism. Not merely utopian, prudential personalism looks forward to the completion and perfection of human nature as it is called to by the divine nature.

Ashley and O'Rourke describe prudential personalism as a "teleological, natural law ethics based on what we now know of human nature and its integral fulfillment through intelligent and free choices."[27]

This methodology is "personalist" insofar as it acknowledges the common human nature we all share, while also insisting that human nature is instantiated in each of us as distinctive, irreducible, unrepeatable human persons. It is "prudential" insofar as it is practical, goal-seeking, and operates in a situated (rather than situational) context.

The first principle of prudential personalism states: "Do those acts, and only those acts, which are appropriate means to the supreme good of true knowledge and love of God, oneself, and the human community both in time and in eternity."[28]

If we attend to each element of prudential personalism's first principle, we will see that its integration and coherence are in harmony with the requirements of what we have called "thinking intensively"; that is, it conforms to the structure of the Ethical Wedding Cake that we have kept in view throughout this book.

Let's begin by looking at the first few words of the first principle of prudential personalism: "Do those acts, and only those acts...."

In the first half of that segment, we see that prudential personalism is prescriptive. It positively and universally commands. In the second half of that segment, we see that prudential personalism is prohibitive. It expressly and universally forbids.

What we have here is an articulation of a moral methodology that eschews relativism. This is a moral methodology for those who want guidance. It does not, will not,

---

[27] Benedict Ashley, O.P., and Kevin O'Rourke, O.P., *Health Care Ethics: A Theological Analysis*, 4th ed. (Washington, D.C.: Georgetown University Press, 1997), p. 166.

[28] Ibid., p. 171.

and cannot cater to those turning to a moral methodology as a means for excuse-making and rationalizations—unlike the proponents of situationalism, proportionalism and other forms of relativism.

"... which are appropriate means...": Clearly, prudential personalism, while teleological in orientation, is not a form of consequentialism. That is to say, the means do matter. It is a practical methodology, not content to rest with the mere form of morality, unlike the extreme duty-ethics exemplified by Kant. Prudential personalism is truly prudential, insofar as it calls upon the moral agent to act in the practical domain, linking means to ends. Prudential personalism does not, will not, and cannot overlook the how, the what, and the why of moral action; nor will it ignore the multi-dimensional human nature of the moral agent.

"... to the supreme good...": These words acknowledge that there is a hierarchy of morality that is intelligible and imperative. There is a moral supreme good because human persons instantiate a universal and identifiable human nature that can and ought to be realized, fulfilled, completed, and perfected by right action. Absent such a human nature, there is no moral hierarchy; any sense or semblance of priority, then, is always and merely arbitrary.

"... of true knowledge and love...": What is morally relevant is intelligible and accessible. It is morally obliging and humanly liberating (liberating in the sense that it frees human individuals from error, illusion, addiction, and impulsiveness). What is morally relevant can be known as such, chosen as such (in other words, it can be truly loved because it is truly loveable), and acted upon as such (that is, moral truth is a summons to right action).

"... of God, oneself, and the human community...": The reference to knowledge and love of God grounds prudential personalism upon a transcendent/Open System metaphysics, within the world view of theism. The reference to the moral significance of God identifies the Supreme Being as Creator and man as creature. Acknowledging and acting upon these truths, prudential personalism may be characterized by destiny rather than fate, as described by Tinder's work discussed in the chapter on metaphysics.

Let's take the references to oneself and the human community together. First, neither may be considered in separation from God. Each and all humans, as individuals and within every human community, are from God as creatures. Likewise, each and all human individuals and communities, as we will see below, will be accountable to God for the stewardship of the human nature and lives with which they have been entrusted.

The possibility and obligation of true knowledge and love of self in light of prudential personalism are not cancelled by, opposed by, or in intrinsic conflict with true knowledge and love of the human community. Naturally social and naturally limited and incomplete, humans, in order to flourish (the goal of ethics), require properly humane and humanizing communities. The indispensable lessons of human interactions, which include fair play, truth-telling, promise-keeping, delay of gratification, self-defense, self-sacrifice, etc., are best communicated, taught, cultivated, and protected within sound human communities, especially within the natural family. That the right relationship between the human individual and the human community must be worked out is largely a matter of ethics-as-science; how the right relationship is worked out between this particular individual in this particular time and place is largely a matter of ethics-as-art.

The interactivity between human individuals, between an individual and any number of human communities, and between human communities rests upon the composite anthropology discussed in the previous chapter. Moral interaction requires moral agents who can find each other and are capable of moral responsibility, attributability, and accountability.

The moral realism of prudential personalism, in conjunction with composite anthropology and the social dimension of the human condition, together necessitate what Western civilization identified as the "cardinal virtues", namely, prudence, fortitude, temperance, and justice.[29] They are called "cardinal" in relation to the Latin word *cardo*, meaning "hinge". As a door hangs upon hinges, so the moral life hangs upon these virtues.

Because ethics is a practical discipline, linking means to ends, choosing the midpoint between excess and defect, applying universal principles to particular situations, the moral life cannot be lived well without the virtue of prudence. It is the virtue that guides the moral agent in the exercise of concrete moral acts.

Subject to pains, difficulties, fears, and vulnerabilities (up to and including death), human life cannot be lived well without the virtue of fortitude. Fortitude is a defense of moral priorities and the hierarchy of goods—preserving the moral agent (or the moral community) from surrendering higher goods to lesser goods. Aided by fortitude, the moral agent can suffer and make sacrifices, even the sacrifice of his own life, so that he does not lose the greatest good, which is the fulfillment of his human nature by living a life in such a way that he is ready for communion with the divine nature after death.

Capable of intense, distracting, beguiling, and even addictive pleasures, human life cannot be lived well without

---

[29] See Josef Pieper's *Four Cardinal Virtues* (Notre Dame, Ind.: University of Notre Dame Press, 1966), a book that is at once accessible and magisterial.

the virtue of temperance. Temperance acknowledges and accepts pleasures as enjoyable accompaniments, while securing the moral life from the danger of allowing pleasures to become disproportionate or even imperious.

Inherently social, human life is lived in interaction with others, in conjunction with communities of various compositions, intimacies, and numbers. What one individual owes to and expects from another individual, what one individual owes to and expects from a community, what a community owes to and expects from an individual, and what various communities owe to and expect from one another—these relations are within the purview of the virtue of justice, so that to each may be rendered his due. Human life cannot be lived well without the virtue of justice. Absent justice, social life will become dehumanizing, as seen in tyrannies, and will ultimately become anti-human when the "Law of the Jungle" holds sway. Guided by justice, humans and their communities may ask of themselves as individuals and as communities, "Are we building a moral house in which we would want to live?"

"... in time and in eternity ..." Regarding the temporal dimension of metaphysics, prudential personalism situates the Human Present of the moral life within the horizons of the Open System. Human nature has its absolute origin in God, the supremely good, wise, generous, and provident Supreme Being. Human nature, designed by God, is instantiated in individuals who are at once unique, irreducible, and unrepeatable, each and all equally human, and who live across the Human Present impelled by an *entelechia*, that drive for fulfillment, that impetus toward the *telos*, which is the full realization, completion, and perfection of human nature. So understood, the authentic moral life includes the common good, individual immortality, and the ultimate moral sanction, who is God. These distinct yet interrelated elements merit further reflection.

Human dignity is rooted in its divine origin and divine terminus. The creating God, infinitely generous and good, making creatures like himself, insofar as they are rational, free, and therefore moral, can only want what is best for these morally capable and morally significant creatures. Infinitely wise and therefore provident, the creating God knows that what is best for his human creatures is himself—precisely because they can know what is true, love what is good, and enjoy what is beautiful. Provident, God has created a moral universe in which human moral agents can move through time and enter eternity, so that they are able to attain the end for which they are made, namely, himself.

This provident arrangement of union with God by moral action, or unfitness for union with God by immoral action, provides the ultimate sanction for ethics. The problem of evil, for those now living in time, includes those instances of good moral agents and actions going apparently unrewarded or otherwise treated unjustly over the course of time. Likewise, we are aware of malefactors who appear to go unpunished and seem even to prosper by their wicked deeds.

The atemporal nature of God and the immortality of the human soul together have the field of eternity within which to find ultimate sanction for virtue and vice, moral success and moral failure, and so work out the problem of evil beyond the familiar bonds of time and space.

Allow me a slight digression to illustrate this point. In April 2018, author Stefan Molyneux made public a video review[30] of the movie *Chappaquiddick*. The movie is an account of a notorious tragedy. On July 18, 1969, U.S. Senator Ted Kennedy drives his car off of a bridge on

---

[30] https://www.youtube.com/watch?v=-619G-sjz7E.

Massachusetts' Chappaquiddick Island. The accident results in the death of passenger Mary Jo Kopechne, a twenty-eight-year-old campaign strategist who worked for Kennedy. Evidence indicates that he left her to drown, while he used money, power, and influence to gloss over his role and her death—thereby securing more money, power, and influence.

Molyneux has described himself as a childhood Christian who philosophized his way into atheism. He admits at the outset of his video that, after watching this movie, he is at something of a crossroads. If what we here call God as the ultimate moral sanction, which Molyneux associates with his childhood Christian faith, is not true, then he admits that he must conclude that Kennedy's actions must be praiseworthy. That is to say, what Kennedy did was the smart thing to do. Had Kennedy taken responsibility for the death of Kopechne (and the sordid events immediately prior to her death), his political career likely would have been over, and he would have suffered a corresponding loss in money, power, and influence. Acting as he did, however, he suffered, not a loss, but a gain in money, power, and influence.

Molyneux admits in his movie review that if there is no ultimate sanction, if there is no immaterial and atemporal means for righting wrongs, rewarding the virtuous, and punishing the vicious, then there is no basis for criticizing, much less for condemning, Kennedy and his actions. Rather than being viewed as a moral reprobate, Kennedy is celebrated as a hero ("the last lion of the Senate")—Aristotle's "crafty man" who gamed the system and came out ahead.

On this view, what else can be said, save that Kennedy won and Kopechne lost? The moral of this story (if one could call it that) is: "Be a Kennedy; don't be a Kopechne!"

What Molyneux's review illustrates for us is that moral realism (that is, "real philosophy for real people") can be found only within the temporal horizon of the Open System, within the world view of theism. The only consistent alternative is the moral nihilism of Nietzsche, embodied by the boundless and unaccountable will-to-power of Ted Kennedy. To put the issue more succinctly, we would do well to recall the observation of Dostoyevsky: "If there is no God, everything is permissible."

This vignette of Molyneux's movie review helps us to see that ethics is an all-or-nothing issue. All the elements must be present and in right relation. Recalling what we said earlier in this work regarding the Open System and the passage of time into eternity, we can see that the Open System allows for ultimate sanction as well as redemptive suffering. Had Kennedy been a virtuous theist, he could have seen that taking responsibility for his actions might cost him dearly but would be well worth the price in terms of the formation of his character and the attainment of his destiny. Apart from the Open System, we could only see Kennedy as praiseworthy-because-effective and Kopechne as an incidental casualty.

A sound ethics is expressed (and may be lived well) by the moral methodology of prudential personalism. Such a moral life must include what Western civilization has always considered indispensable to moral life, namely, the cardinal virtues.

Antecedent to that ethics is a composite anthropology. Composite anthropology grounds the dynamics of responsibility, attributability, and accountability. Absent any of these, there can be no ethics.

Likewise, composite anthropology, exemplified by philosophical sacramentality and the Funnel Concept of the Body, ground the transition of relation-to-object (I-It) to relation-to-subject (I-You), to relation-to-intimate (I-Thou). Apart from these, there is no ethics.

Antecedent to that anthropology is a transcendent/Open System metaphysics. This allows for an immaterial human privacy, a responsible source of moral action. Not subject to decay, the immaterial human privacy continues into eternity, oriented toward a divine *telos* and subject to a divine ultimate sanction. Apart from the world view of theism, these metaphysical antecedents of ethics are not possible. Consequently, morality has metaphysical and divine requirements.

The rightly ordered Ethical Wedding Cake constitutes the antecedents of a sound morality. The supports of prudential personalism include common sense as well as ordinary human experience across times, locations, and cultures. These supports are buttressed by philosophical reflection within the Western natural law tradition, going back at least to ancient Greece.

The objections to prudential personalism have been seen and overcome throughout the course of our examination of the alternatives of world views, metaphysics, anthropology, and ethics. What are the consequents of endorsing and living prudential personalism?

To answer that question, let's turn to the Moral Equation, first spoken of in this work in chapter 5:

$$\text{Moral Equation}$$
$$RV^2 \rightarrow RD^2 \rightarrow RM \rightarrow RE \overset{\displaystyle UD}{\wedge}$$

where R = right/rightly (rational); D = desire (nonrational);
M = means (practical); E = ends (practical);
UD = ultimate destiny (metaphysical/transcendent)

Rightly value what is rightly valuable so as to rightly desire what is rightly desirable so as to choose the right means to the right end and thus achieve one's ultimate destiny (*telos*).

The Moral Equation is a linear depiction of the dynamics of the Fundamental Conjoint Disjunct. It is also a formulaic expression of the first principle of prudential personalism.

If we decompose the Moral Equation into its basic elements, we will see the comprehensive and coherent character of prudential personalism and the Ethical Wedding Cake it rests upon, along with the world view of theism in which it resides. The analysis of the component parts of the Moral Equation, along with the relations that exist among them, include the opportunity to know and live a truly human and humanizing science and art of ethics that can do justice to human individuals and communities. The *entelechia* within human nature is from God. The *telos* that completes human nature is God. The path from one to the other is the moral life lived well. That moral life may be understood, explained, guided, and lived well by the methodology of prudential personalism.

All of the "rightly"s and "right"s of the Moral Equation appeal to the reason/logic aspect of the Fundamental Conjoint Disjunct. They are indications of ethics-as-science.

"Rightly value what is rightly valuable" is a function of the knowing subject to know what is objectively true, within an orderly, meaningful, consistent, and intelligible system. It is an essential function of conscience to conform the intellect of the knowing subject to the objectively true.

To "rightly desire what is rightly desirable" draws upon the affect/imagination point of the Fundamental Conjoint Disjunct. It is the work of a rational and free moral agent to know what is good and to respond to it with rightly ordered desire and anticipation, orienting oneself toward what is good precisely because it is good. If the properly functioning intellect is the eye that is open to the light of what is truly good, the properly functioning will is an appetite (one might also say "affection" or "passion") for the good, freely moving toward the true good that alone will satisfy that appetite.

Ethics is a practical rather than speculative discipline, and purposeful actions must be undertaken. The work of the moral agent is to be more than merely effective. That is, the work of the moral agent is to do more than simply link useful means to desired ends. What the moral agent seeks, and how he seeks it, is of moral significance. Morally speaking, he may not choose just any ends, for he has a nature, of which some ends are worthy and satisfying and others not. Likewise, the ends do not justify any and every means. Succeeding in business may be praiseworthy; murdering your rival to do so never is.

The realization of right ends does not constitute an end in itself. As seen above, the moral life requires an ultimate sanction, an application of just deserts that is imposed beyond the reach of the material and the temporal. Reference to ultimate sanction entails the Moral Equation's reference to an ultimate destiny (using the work of Tinder in earlier chapters as a frame of reference).

The human person, as intelligent and free, is oriented toward what is true, what is good, and what is beautiful. The human privacy is immaterial and so cannot be satisfied, cannot come to rest, in what is material and temporal and therefore limited. It is inevitable for the human person on this side of eternity to ask, "Is that all there is? What else is there?" The human person is oriented to be satisfied only by Truth itself, Goodness itself, Beauty itself—and these in unlimited, unrestricted modes. In other words, human life is completed and perfected only in union with what the Western tradition has understood to be the Supreme Being, the locus and unity of all perfections.

The moral life lived through time is a preparation of one's capacities for union with the True, the Good, and the Beautiful. Human individuals succeed or fail as human precisely to the degree that they have lived moral lives that open them to see, desire, move toward, embrace, and receive the True, the Good, and the Beautiful. Likewise, human communities succeed or fail to the degree that they generate and foster such moral agents.

The moral life envisioned by the Moral Equation, guided by prudential personalism, is a path to perfection for moral agents who are embodied, intelligent, free, social, virtuous, and immortal. Sadly, it must be acknowledged that such a position these days is very much in the minority. Relativism, emotivism, and nihilism of various kinds, combinations, and degrees of sophistication constitute the view of the majority at this time. One purpose of this book is to provide its readers with a flashlight, map, and compass so that individuals and communities can find their way through this present darkness.

CHAPTER 7

EPILOGUE

The rule of no realm is mine, neither of Gondor nor any
other, great or small. But all worthy things that are in peril
as the world now stands, those are my care. And for my
part, I shall not wholly fail of my task, though Gondor
should perish, if anything passes through this night that
can still grow fair or bear fruit and flower again in days to
come. For I also am a steward. Did you not know?

— J.R.R. Tolkien, *The Return of the King*

I have often told my students that one of the great challenges for a teacher, a writer, or a speaker is to finish by
addressing the questions, "So what?" and "Who cares?" I
also tell them, "And if you're really good, you'll take on
the question, 'Now what?'"

The quote from Tolkien gives us some insight into
all three questions. Like the wizard Gandalf into whose
mouth Tolkien put the words cited above, we too now
live in a world where "worthy things are in peril". We
cannot afford to get moral evaluation wrong; likewise,
we cannot afford to ignore or be silent before the errors we
see and hear. To fail in this task is to allow the lights to go
out. That answers the question, "So what?"

Addressing the Steward of the Kingdom of Gondor,
Gandalf admits that he himself is also a steward. Those

who count on him cannot afford to have him fail or be feckless. Likewise, every steward will be called to account for the stewardship he exercised over the goods entrusted to his care. Our neighbor and our posterity and our ancestors will take note of what we do and fail to do. And theism assures us that God will provide the just and certain ultimate sanction for our actions and inactions. That answers the question, "Who cares?"

The rest of this chapter addresses the question, "Now what?"

It is praiseworthy to seek, know, admire, love, proclaim, and conform to Truth. This process of "Truth-ing", far from being esoteric, ethereal, or exceptional, has a wide-ranging, deep, universal, and practical import. Consider this note of caution from the French economist Frédéric Bastiat: "When misguided public opinion honors what is despicable and despises what is honorable, punishes virtue and rewards vice, encourages what is harmful and discourages what is useful, applauds falsehood and smothers truth under indifference or insult, a nation turns its back on progress and can be restored only by the terrible lessons of catastrophe."

One reason I wrote this book was to help forestall or lessen, if not fully avoid, the "terrible lessons of catastrophe" sure to befall our present times and posterity as a natural (and supernatural) consequence of favoring the despicable over the honorable, the vicious over the virtuous. Over the years, so many have told me that they had seen or heard something that they intuited as not right but could not quite articulate the whys and hows of what was wrong and to be rejected and what was right and to be pursued. One purpose of this book is to give people of honesty, thoughtfulness, and goodwill—especially those surrounded by hucksters, propagandists, bullies, and those who are just plain wrong—a set of tools for detecting and refuting error. These same tools can be used for identifying, proclaiming, and living for the True, the Good, and the Beautiful. In so doing, this book is simply recapitulating for our time and posterity what Saint Thomas Aquinas (adapting Aristotle) spoke of as the "Office of the Wise Man": "It belongs to one and the same science, however, both to pursue one of two contraries and to oppose the other. Medicine, for example, seeks to effect health and to eliminate illness. Hence, just as it belongs to the wise man to meditate especially on the truth belonging to the first principle and to teach it to others, so it belongs to him to refute the opposing falsehood."[1]

This book was written to teach truth and to help others to teach truth. Likewise, it was written to oppose falsehood and to teach others to oppose falsehood.

To sum up how I now understand this book, I find it irresistible to mix metaphors. One might say that this book offers a taxonomy of errors and a summary of truth. One might make use of the popular acronym "EDC" ("Everyday Carry"), or, as the advertisements for American Express used to say, "Don't leave home without it!" Real philosophy for real people is a set of portable and adaptable tools that you can always keep with you, "on your belt", so to speak, like a Leatherman multitool or a Swiss army knife.

Looked at another way, we can see this book as facilitating moral reasoning, moral discourse, and moral action, along the full range of the parallel continua of education described at the outset of this work. From the most public and formal context to the most private and informal

---

[1] Saint Thomas Aquinas, *Summa Contra Gentiles*, trans. Anton C. Pegis (South Bend, Ind.: University of Notre Dame Press, 1975), bk. 1, chap. 1, no. 3.

context, those who make use of this book need not be lost, led astray, or badgered into silence.

Paul Weiss told me that a key test of any philosophy is: "Can it be lived?" I am confident that the philosophy outlined and recommended in this book can be lived. An honest examination of the Western moral tradition, drawing upon its record of history, philosophy, theology, literature, and the arts, will show a rich array of those who lived in harmony with the moral realism described here. Individuals and communities have already practiced what Josef Pieper called the "selfless self-preservation" of a virtuous life, living—often at the cost of great sacrifice—in light of and for true knowledge and love of God, self, and neighbor. Alas, that same honest examination of Western civilization is replete with examples of individuals and communities who were inhuman, dehumanizing, and finally self-destructive, by means of rejecting the summons, obligations, and heights of the human vocation.

This work, a contemporary restatement of the long tradition of moral realism, is also meant to be a challenge to every human individual and community. I have made a habit of urging my students to work with one eye on the horizon, knowing full well that allies, antagonists, the uncertain, and the indifferent are moving toward you. You need to be ready for them all. Those are the people we will face. What of the choices we will face? The starkness of the choices was set in sharp relief by Colombian author Nicolás Gómez Dávila: "If one does not believe in God, the only honest alternative is vulgar utilitarianism. The rest is rhetoric."[2]

---

[2] Nicolás Gómez Dávila, *Escolios a un texto implícito: Selección* (Bogota, Colombia: Villegas Editores, 2001), p. 474.

In other words, we must recognize that we need God in order to be good and that true humanity requires real divinity. Are we prepared to accept those facts? Knowing that we need God to be good and resolved to act accordingly in a world that now insists on the contrary while silencing or even killing the non-compliant, we would do well to take as our rallying cry these stirring words of Aleksandr Solzhenitsyn: "You can resolve to live your life with integrity. Let your credo be this: Let the lie come into the world. Let it even triumph. But not through me."[3] You and everyone you know are being lied to and are being asked to participate in the lie. This book can help you to name the lie, tell the truth, live the truth, and teach others to do the same. And therefore I close by asking you: "Now what?"

[3] From Aleksandr Solzhenitsyn's Nobel Lecture, quoted in Jay Nordlinger, "A Life and an Example", *National Review*, December 17, 2018, https://www.nationalreview.com/2018/12/remembering-alexander-solzhenitsyn-a-life-and-example/.

AFTERWORD

by Robert J. Spitzer, S.J.

Robert McTeigue, S.J., provides an essential readable "tool kit" to help today's readers assess and critique the many competing philosophies proffered through the classroom, media, and culture, so that they might learn to think, love, and act according to the truth. Written for ordinary folks, the book does not demand of its readers any formal academic training or any nuanced philosophical vocabulary. Rather, it builds from the ground up, always teaching, explaining, and unpacking. Yet for all the book's simplicity, it manages to touch the recesses of metaphysical and moral thought, and it provides a powerful, systematic analysis of the chief world views that shape and color human behavior. This more technical afterword will give a kind of aerial view of *Real Philosophy for Real People* in the wider landscape of science and academic philosophy, showing the broad scope of McTeigue's project and suggesting some further reading for those wish to continue expanding their toolbox.

Sadly, the vast majority of the postmodern philosophies encountered in our culture deceive their prospective adherents into unsubstantiated self-destructive beliefs such as naturalism, the omniscience of science, metaphysical materialism, anthropological reductionism, and ethical relativism. These destructive beliefs move beyond individuals into personal relationships, communities, and the culture, which has a catastrophic effect presciently summarized by the nineteenth-century French economist Frédéric Bastiat:

> When misguided public opinion honors what is despicable and despises what is honorable, punishes virtue and rewards vice, encourages what is harmful and discourages what is useful, applauds falsehood and smothers truth under indifference or insult, a nation turns its back on progress and can be restored only by the terrible lessons of catastrophe.[1]

These philosophies cannot hope to provide a path to truth and goodness—a path to the flourishing of self, of others, of culture, and of society, because as we shall see, they are excessively narrow and radically incomplete. They reduce metaphysics to mere physics and reduce human nature to mere embodiment, which reduces us to a shadow of our former selves. This diminishment has ruinous consequences for ethics—living a good life toward human flourishing. When these philosophies are seen through the lens of McTeigue's typology of world views, metaphysics, anthropology, and ethics, they are exposed as imposters—giving half-truths, deceptive moral prescripts, and undervaluation of human nature, dignity, fulfillment, and destiny. If they are believed by our culture over the long term, we can fully expect Bastiat's catastrophe. McTeigue's tool kit offers a realistic, accessible way out of this destructive path by systematically showing what we should know and do to live a good life, assess philosophical claims, and critique rival philosophies for our sake and the sake of our neighbor and culture.

---

[1] Fréderic Bastiat, *Economic Harmonies*, trans. W. Hayden Boyers (Irvington-on-Hudson, NY: Foundation for Economic Education, 1996), p. 517.

How does McTeigue's typological analysis work? What is its underlying logic? In his words:

> Absent a clear account of what a human person is, there can be no hope of identifying human flourishing (such flourishing is the goal of ethics) or of identifying the means toward that end. Likewise, an anthropology cannot stand unless it is built upon a thorough account of the real—in terms of both reality's elements and its temporal horizons—and that is the goal of a sound metaphysics. Absent the foundation that only a thorough and coherent metaphysics can provide, an account of ethics can only be a collection of mere assertions and surmises inferred from hollow or partial premises. Metaphysics and anthropology provide the fixed compass points by which ethics must navigate; real individuals and communities must make the actual trek toward human fulfillment.[2]

Though McTeigue uses great stories, humor, and commonsense definitions to illustrate his many insights, readers should be aware that he is profoundly integrative and systematic, which is essential to his purpose. I will dedicate the rest of this afterword to giving a roadmap of his architectonic efforts. The following table shows his integration of world views, metaphysics, and philosophical anthropology and the ethical consequences following from them. The concepts used in the table are explained in Table 1.

World View

First, we look at world view, column one. McTeigue provides a concise explanation of James Sire's *The Universe Next Door*. The vertical movement down the column represents the historical and conceptual degradation arising out

---

[2] Chapter 6, pp. 201–2.

Table 1: World Views

World View	Metaphysics	Philosophical Anthropology	Ethical Consequences
Theism: *Ultimate transcendent principle which is personal and absolute truth, goodness, and beauty.*	Ultimate personal, transcendent reality, transcendent origin, and fulfillment. Time is not a closed system—an eternal future. Absolute truth, goodness, and beauty, which implies a personal God.	Human beings have public (bodily) and private (trans-physical self-consciousness and inwardness—a soul) dimensions. Nondualistic permeability allows for human freedom. Immateriality of soul allows for survival of consciousness after bodily death.	Transcendent metaphysics allows for an ultimate and eternal fulfillment of human nature through perfect truth, goodness, and beauty. Open future allows for eternal consequences. Reality of a transphysical soul plus permeability (nondualism) allows for human freedom to be responsible, attributable, and accountable. Most complete assessment of human nature for derivation of ethical principles.
Deism: *Ultimate transcendent principle, but not personal.*	Ultimate metaphysical transcendent principle is not personal and may not be perfect truth, goodness, and beauty. As impersonal, it manifests no love or providence.	Deism is open to a human soul. If so, then possible survival of bodily death and potential for free choice. If no soul, then no survival or freedom.	*Uncertainty* about God as absolute truth, goodness, beauty, and love, and uncertainty about life after death and human freedom leads to uncertainty about responsibility, attributability, and accountability. Less complete and more ambiguous understanding of human nature for derivation of ethical principles.

Naturalism (and nihilism): *Truth and goodness come through science—limited to physical universe and physical processes—not absolute.* (N.B.: Naturalism devolves to nihilism, because naturalism lives and dies with the human body and the physical universe alone—we are but mere pain-pleasure assimilators.)	Materialism/physicalism—no God, no eternal destiny—closed system. Physical reality exhausts the whole of reality.	Physical reductionism. No soul, implying no interior self-consciousness and awareness of transcendent truth and goodness. Therefore, reduction to physical/bodily stimulus-response. Therefore, deterministic—no real freedom.	No God, no soul, and no awareness of transcendent truth and goodness implies no eternal future, no human freedom, and no objective morality. No freedom implies no possibility of responsibility, attributability, and accountability. Human nature is reduced to physics-biology, which reduces ethics to pain-pleasure utilitarianism or subjective situationism/emotivism.
Postmodernism: *Truth and goodness are social constructs—not objective, but subjective agreement within a group. Deconstruction of the linguistic-social constructions of the powerful is the best we can do.*	There is no "knowable reality" in postmodernism; therefore, there is no metaphysics. God, an eternal future, and even the physical world are, in principle, unknowable. All metaphysical/physical theories are sociolinguistic constructions of the powerful that must be deconstructed and exposed.	Since there is no knowable reality, there is also no knowable human nature. We do not discover what human nature really is, but we only give meaning to humanity through our social constructions. You "are" what you and your group declare yourself to be. Therefore, real human freedom is illusory, but your group can declare that they have some.	Since there is no real truth or goodness, no knowable God, no knowable human nature, no knowable human freedom, then there can be no basis for objective principles in ethics. Ethics is a mere socially constructed convention that can be deconstructed. Right and wrong is what your group's social construction makes it out to be.

of the loss (or rejection) of God. The movement from theism to deism to naturalism-nihilism and to postmodernism was almost inevitable because the unjustified rejection of an ultimate efficient and final cause (God) leaves everything between origin and finality unmoored, undefined, and unguided. Naturalism, which grounds the whole of reality and human nature in physical processes, cannot possibly bear the weight of lost transcendent purpose and absolute truth and goodness. Human reason, the champion of scientific naturalism, could not bring ultimate truth (complete intelligibility) and perfect goodness out of mere physicality, for it cannot break out of its physical self-limitation.

As can be seen from the table, the decline of world view has significant metaphysical, anthropological, and ethical consequences that affect our ability to find meaning in (or in the case of postmodernism, give meaning to) life, self, others, and goodness. This has led to the despair of ultimate, absolute, and transcendent truth and goodness, which has led to everything from confusion to chaos in world culture. Little wonder that the suicide rates of young people have increased 56 percent in just ten years (2007–2017)[3] and depression rates have increased by 63 percent in eight years (2009–2017) among young adults (eighteen to twenty-five).[4]

Metaphysics

We now proceed to metaphysics (column two). McTeigue defines metaphysics as follows: "an attempt at a systematic

---

[3] This figure comes from the Center for Disease Control and Prevention (2019). Brianna Abbott, "Youth Suicide Rate Increased 56% in Decade, CDC Says", *Wall Street Journal*, October 17, 2019.

[4] Jean M. Twenge et al., "Age, Period, and Cohort Trends in Mood Disorder Indicators and Suicide-Related Outcomes in a Nationally Representative Dataset, 2005–2017", *Journal of Abnormal Psychology* 128, no. 3 (2019): 185–99. This study focused on 200,000 young adults over an eight-year period.

and comprehensive account of what is first and final, what is primordially and ultimately real, an explanation of what is and why the real is as it is."[5]

As can be seen from the above table, theism gives the fullest account of metaphysics, anthropology, and ethics. Though theism presents limits for anthropology and ethics, the move to materialism/physicalism (and the acceleration of physicalist thinking in some quarters of science and philosophy) led to the cultural demise of ultimate reality (i.e., an uncaused reality existing through itself that can explain the whole of reality[6]). This loss of ultimate reality led to the further demise of immateriality, and hence of a transcendent soul. At this juncture, metaphysics, if we can call it that, was left with mere materialism—mere physical substances and processes which, because of their intrinsic limits, cannot explain objective truth (let alone ultimate objective truth), goodness (let alone ultimate goodness), and freedom. As will be explained below, this also led to the demise of anthropology and ethics.

As McTeigue shows, materialism is an evidently weak and incomplete ontological position and really cannot even explain our capacity for scientific inquiry (to which materialists often appeal). Sir Arthur Eddington, one of the world's greatest astrophysicists, recognized that scientific inquiry about physics had to be transphysical (spiritual), putting it this way:

> We all know that there are regions of the human spirit untrammeled by the world of physics. In the mystic sense of the creation around us, in the expression of art, in a

---

[5] Chapter 4, p. 107.

[6] This theistic ultimate reality is proven by philosopher Bernard Lonergan in chapter 19 of his work *Insight: A Study of Human Understanding. Collected Works of Bernard Lonergan*, vol. 3, ed. Frederick E. Crowe and Robert M. Doran (Toronto: University of Toronto Press, 1992).

yearning towards God, the soul grows upward and finds the fulfillment of something implanted in its nature. The sanction for this development is within us, a striving born with our consciousness or an Inner Light proceeding from a greater power than ours. Science can scarcely question this sanction, for the pursuit of science springs from a striving which the mind is impelled to follow, a questioning that will not be suppressed. Whether in the intellectual pursuits of science or in the mystical pursuits of the spirit, the light beckons ahead and the purpose surging in our nature responds.[7]

McTeigue presents an astute argument against *atomistic* materialism, but readers seeking a refutation of the "field view" of materialism—where reality is reduced to space-time fields, quantum fields, plasma fields, quantum cosmological configurations, etc.—may want to look at the evidence for three transmaterial realities that are necessary for physical reality in all its forms (e.g., universes, multiverses, and physical, chemical, and biological laws and structures):

1. *Time.* The transcendent mentative (thinking) reality unifying "earlier and later" within a single magnitude. Henri Bergson presents a probative proof of what he calls "transcendent elementary memory" (or "elementary consciousness") to do this.[8]
2. *Complete intelligibility of being.* Bernard Lonergan proves the complete intelligibility of reality, entailing

[7] Sir Arthur Eddington, *The Nature of the Physical World* (Cambridge: Cambridge University Press, 1929), pp. 327–28.

[8] Henri Bergson, *The Creative Mind: An Introduction to Metaphysics* (New York: Dover, 2010). See also Bergson's *Duration and Simultaneity*, trans. Leon Jacobson (Indianapolis: Bobbs-Merrill Company, 1963).

a unique unrestricted act of thinking that is the ultimate cause of the rest of reality.[9]

3. *An uncaused reality.* It can be logically demonstrated
   that without at least one uncaused reality, the whole
   of reality would be nothing. Contemporary Thom-
   istic proofs can further demonstrate that such an
   uncaused reality must be unrestricted, and therefore unique, making it the one ultimate cause of
   all reality.[10]

If complete intelligibility and an uncaused reality are
necessary for anything at all (material or immaterial) to
exist, and if time is required for physical reality to exist,
and if these three realities entail not only transcendent
intelligence but a unique unrestricted ground of all reality, then the denial of God (and its metaphysical, anthropological, and ethical consequences) would not only be
unnecessary, but utterly false. The consequences of such a
false denial of God are so serious that it would be foolish
to ignore the contemporary arguments and studies mentioned above. If they ground reasonable and responsible
belief in God, then we must separate ourselves from the
contemporary naturalistic/materialistic world view (and its
nihilistic and postmodern cousins), affirm God, and investigate the anthropological and ethical consequences of
theism. This could be the most important investigation
of your life.

[9] Lonergan, *Insight.* For a logical summary of this proof, see Robert Spitzer,
"A Contemporary Metaphysical Proof of the Existence of God", *International
Philosophical Quarterly* 59, no. 4 (2019): 427–66.

[10] For a contemporary demonstration of this, see Robert Spitzer *New Proofs
for the Existence of God: Contributions of Contemporary Physics and Philosophy*
(Grand Rapids, MI: Eerdmans, 2010), ch. 3. See also Spitzer, "A Contemporary Metaphysical Proof".

Philosophical Anthropology

We may now proceed to philosophical anthropology (column 3). McTeigue demonstrates the need for a transcendent principle (like a self-conscious soul) to explain the "who" of the human body. It is hard to defend a materialistic view of the human person in light of this argument. For readers interested in additional contemporary studies that validate his argument through the methodologies of natural science and philosophy of mind, you might refer to the following works:

1. *The Character of Consciousness* by David Chalmers—a New York University professor's comprehensive assessment of the "hard problem of consciousness", showing the insufficiency of physical processes to explain conscious experience and self-awareness[11]
2. Peer-reviewed medical studies of transphysical consciousness (for example, in near-death experiences), which show the insufficiency of materialism to explain the presence of consciousness after clinical death[12]
3. *Evolution of the Brain: Creation of the Self* by Sir John Eccles—a Nobel Prize–winning physiologist and

---

[11] David Chalmers, *The Character of Consciousness* (Oxford: Oxford University Press, 2010).

[12] Pim van Lommel et al., "Near-Death Experience in Survivors of Cardiac Arrest: A Prospective Study in the Netherlands", *The Lancet*, 358, no. 9298 (2001): 2039–45; Sam Parnia et al., "AWARE—Awareness during Resuscitation—A Prospective Study", *Journal of Resuscitation* 85, no. 12 (2014). For an extensive list of references to medical studies of near-death experiences and transphysical implications of consciousness, see Robert Spitzer, *The Soul's Upward Yearning: Clues to Transcendent Nature from Experience and Reason* (San Francisco: Ignatius Press, 2015), pp. 173–203. For a study of the insufficiency of physicalist explanations of near-death experiences and consciousness, see Mario Beauregard, *Brain Wars: The Scientific Battle over the Existence of the Mind and the Proof That Will Change the Way We Live* (New York: Harper One, 2012).

philosopher's study of the transphysical nature of
human identity and consciousness[13]

After showing the need for a transmaterial view of the
human person, McTeigue confronts the problem of dualism (division between body and mind/soul). McTeigue,
using Paul Weiss, reveals the falsity of dualism through an
inference of permeability between the public (bodily/out-
ward) dimension and the private (self-conscious/inward)
dimension of persons. Without such permeability, the
human being would not be able to move from inwardness
(the "I" or "who" of self-consciousness) to an outward
public act—or move from the public (bodily) domain to
the private ("I" or "who" of self-consciousness). But we
clearly do, and the evidence comes from dualists themselves. As McTeigue notes, "Dualists are already in contact
with what they claim they cannot find or reach or they
would not be able to lament the separation from which
they claim to suffer."[14] This ingenious argument is supported by several philosophical–physiological studies of Sir
John Eccles and colleagues.

The problem of dualism is not merely abstract. Failure to respond to it undermines the possibility of human
freedom and therefore the possibility of being ethical.
McTeigue shows that ethics presupposes responsibility,
attributability, and accountability, defined in chapter 4,
which in turn requires interaction between the private
(inward "I" of self-consciousness) needed for freedom, and
the public (outward) body needed to affect the outside

[13] John Eccles, *Evolution of the Brain: Creation of the Self* (London: Routledge,
1989). Eccles' approach correlates well with McTeigue's argument.

[14] Eccles' *Evolution of the Brain*. See also John Eccles, "A Unitary Hypothesis
of Mind-Brain Interaction in the Cerebral Cortex", *Proceedings of the Royal
Society of London (Biological Sciences)*, no. 1299 (1990): 433–51.

world. Inasmuch as this interaction does occur, as shown above, then human beings can be responsible, attributable, and accountable for their free choices.

Ethical Consequences

With theistic metaphysical and anthropological realism justified, McTeigue proceeds to an assessment of major ethical positions developed throughout the history of philosophy. His aim is first to show the necessity of a *theistic* metaphysics to ground absolute objective truth and goodness, and of a transcendent, nondualistic human nature to ground human freedom and our capacity to apprehend that objective truth and goodness. If the evidence for theistic metaphysics and transcendent anthropology (given above) is probative, then it is incumbent upon us to find ethical methods commensurate with and worthy of absolute truth and goodness as well as our freedom and transcendent nature.

McTeigue presents several potential candidates for such ethical methods:

- *Deontology*—duty to act in accordance with a lawgiver, with various candidates for this role of "lawgiver", e.g., God, self, or state/culture
- *Utilitarianism*—assessment of goodness on the basis of pain-pleasure or benefits-deficits in the consequences
- *Nature-Virtue Ethics*—acting according to the highest capacities of human nature (which vitally depends on our definition of "human nature")

Before examining these major approaches to ethics, McTeigue gives the three major determinants for evaluating ethical systems. He is looking for the ethical system that best assesses these three criteria:

1. The moral quality of an action
2. The agent's intention in performing the action (intending good or evil)
3. The circumstances of the agent[15]

McTeigue gives important extended critiques of the above ethical systems based on their failure to consider one or more of the above three criteria as well as the negative outcomes they may have on individuals, the culture, and society. McTeigue begins with *deontology*, showing a high emphasis on criterion 2 (the intention of the agent), but almost no attention on criterion 1 (the moral quality of the action) or criterion 3 (the circumstances of the agent's situation). He goes on to describe the personal and cultural problems arising out of divinely based deontology (God as the lawgiver), state-based deontology (the state as the lawgiver), and Kantian deontology (the duty to obey the demands of universalizable interior imperatives). The list of problems with these deontological views ranges from religious fanaticism and terrorism to autocratic and totalitarian states and to the emptiness of abstract Kantian formalism.

McTeigue also criticizes utilitarian—or consequentialist— and situationist systems, because they focus almost exclusively on criterion 3 (circumstances and consequences), but ignore criterion 1 (the moral quality of the action— particularly with respect to the means used to achieve a

[15] "Moral evaluation includes discourse about what are known as the three moral determinants: the moral quality of the act itself; the intention of the moral agent; the circumstances in which the act takes place." Chapter 6, p. 204.

particular end) and criterion 2 (intention). These systems have also led to significant personal and cultural problems, because they run contrary to Saint Augustine's dictum, which is as true today as when he said it: "The end does not justify the means." If any means can be used to maximize benefits and minimize deficits, then economic exploitation and political totalitarianism—such as Stalinism, Maoism, Fascism—and all other forms of political-economic abuse can be justified so long as they will achieve marginal benefits in the end.

This leaves us with an Aristotelian approach to ethics that aims to act according to the highest dimensions of our nature. Aristotle identified four major virtues that can help us reach this highest end of our nature—prudence, justice, fortitude/courage, and temperance.

In this Aristotelian framework of virtue toward optimal use and fulfillment of our nature, it is exceedingly important to have a fully developed philosophical anthropology in order to know the highest dimensions of our nature as well as the metaphysical grounds and potentialities of that nature. This is the point at which McTeigue's architectonic approach to philosophy becomes vital, because an incomplete or minimalistic view of metaphysics—i.e., the whole of reality, including ultimate reality—and of anthropology could lead not only to an underestimation and undervaluation of human dignity, destiny, and fulfillment, but also to a mistreatment of others and society as a whole based on that undervaluation. We do not have to look far to see the consequences of this in Marxist materialism, naturalism (with its tendency toward nihilism), and postmodernism.

If we do not believe that we a have a soul capable of appreciating and desiring perfect truth, goodness, and beauty, if there is no supreme reality of absolute truth, goodness, and beauty, and if there is no future beyond the material world to achieve and enjoy this fulfillment, then we will underlive our lives and underestimate our value as well as the value of everyone else. The historical consequences of this undervaluation of self and others are marked in the tragedies of two world wars, the Stalinist purges, Nazi ethnic cleansing, failed cultural revolutions, and the "paradise" of the Khmer Rouge. As noted above, this underestimation of human nature stands at the root of the hugely increased rates of depression, anxiety, substance abuse, familial tensions, and suicides in the most affluent culture the world has ever known.[16]

So where does this leave us? We need to investigate the best evidence to find a complete and correct metaphysics and anthropology upon which to base our idea of our highest end and the good actions needed to obtain it. If you, the reader, are convinced by McTeigue's arguments against metaphysical and anthropological materialism and the above additional evidence for a supreme being and a transphysical soul, then you will want seriously to consider the ethical system selected by McTeigue to fulfill your nature, to treat others with the same optimal dignity you find in yourself, and to act rightly— *prudential personalism.*

If we affirm the existence of a personal God, a transcendent soul, an open future destiny (unto eternity), permeability between body and soul, and human freedom, then we can simultaneously affirm our nature (and its fulfillment) to be tied to God and *his* will and destiny for us. McTeigue, following Benedict Ashley and Kevin O'Rourke, expresses the first principle of prudential personalism this way: "Do

---

[16] See the 2004 study of the American Psychiatric Association showing that nonreligious affiliation correlates with these five negative conditions. Kanita Dervic et al., "Religious Affiliation and Suicide Attempts", *American Journal of Psychiatry* 161, no. 12 (2004): 2303–8.

those acts, and only those acts, which are appropriate means to the supreme good of true knowledge and love of God, oneself, and the human community, both in time and in eternity."[17] Inasmuch as McTeigue's metaphysical and anthropological conclusions are correct and complete, this ethical principle holds out the potential to actualize our most complete fulfillment, dignity, and interpersonal relationships. It will also give us the guidance and impetus to act rightly toward others, society, and the supreme being.

So how do we know what to do? How do we know what will foster and enhance the knowledge and love of God both now and throughout eternity? We can follow the example of Aristotle and develop the virtues that will lead to the actualization of this principle: prudence, justice, fortitude/courage, and temperance. Yet these alone will not get us to our goal. Knowing and doing what will enhance the love of God and others requires entering into the mind and heart of God, which in turn requires some disclosure—revelation—from him. If our metaphysics and anthropology are correct, and there is a supreme being who is absolute truth and goodness, and he has created us with a transphysical soul that finds its fulfillment in himself, then we must suppose he will give us that revelation so that we might freely follow his will toward that fulfillment.

So where can we find this revelation? This question goes beyond the scope of McTeigue's book, but the groundwork he has laid enables us to give a partial answer. Inasmuch as his anthropology and underlying metaphysics are correct, we should expect to find the first principle

[17]Benedict M. Ashley et al., *Health Care Ethics: A Catholic Theological Analysis*, 5th ed. (Washington, D.C.: Georgetown University Press, 2006), p. 171.

of prudential personalism in every world religion. At this point, Friedrich Heiler's assessment of the seven major characteristics of world religions may prove helpful:

1. The transcendent, the holy, the divine, the Other, is real.
2. The transcendent reality is immanent in human awareness.
3. This transcendent reality is the highest truth, highest good, and highest beauty.
4. This transcendent reality is loving and compassionate—and seeks to reveal its love to human beings.
5. The way to God requires prayer, ethical self-discipline, purgation of self-centeredness, asceticism, and redressing of offenses.
6. The way to God also includes service and responsibility to people.
7. The highest way to eternal bliss in the transcendent reality is through love.[18]

What the seven characteristics do not tell us is the meaning of "good", "love", and "compassion". Variations in the definitions of these central ideas have led to major differences in world religions. So which religion gives the most correct and complete account of these ideas and how to achieve them? Inasmuch as Jesus Christ taught that love is the highest commandment, defined it through the Beatitudes and the parables (such as the good Samaritan and the prodigal son), and demonstrated it in his own actions unto self-sacrificial death on a cross, leading to the Resurrection,

[18] Friedrich Heiler, "The History of Religions as a Preparation for the Cooperation of Religions", in *The History of Religions*, ed. Mircea Eliade and J. Kitagawa (Chicago: University of Chicago Press, 1959), pp. 142–53.

he holds out the potential for being the self-revelation of the all-loving God. In my view, prudential personalism, and the metaphysics and anthropology upon which it is built, draws us into the heart of this revelation that is the culminating moment of McTeigue's architectonic efforts.

ACKNOWLEDGMENTS

Imagine a story that begins like this: "You should write a book about that!" It continues: "You've started a book about that? Great!" Then the story takes a darker turn: "When are you going to finish that book?" Then it gets worse: "Are you *still* working on that book?" Until finally: "Are you *ever* going to finish that book?" Eventually, somehow, the sun begins to shine: "A publisher accepted the book? Great!" Followed by the inevitable: "When is it going to be published?"

The book you are holding in your hands finally saw the light of day because so many people—more than I can count or recall accurately—insisted on asking those questions repeatedly. So here's my imperfect attempt to pay imperfectly my debt of gratitude to all those who helped me to finish the book and get it published: to him who is the way, the truth, the life; to my students who demanded tools to help them know, love, and do the truth; to my family, who has loved me through it all; to the Society of Jesus, for granting me permission to publish this work; to my friends who insisted that I really am a writer, especially Jonnie, David, and Brendan, the most stubborn of them; to my great teachers, who helped inform me and form me and transform me, especially Paul Weiss; to my friends and colleagues at Ignatius Press, who took a stack of papers and a collection of electronic files and turned it all into a book.

I must also acknowledge my profound gratitude to Jesuit Father Robert Spitzer, who wrote a most helpful afterword to this book. I met Father Spitzer many years ago, when I was a layman and we were both in doctoral studies at the Catholic University of America. We both studied under Paul Weiss, and we both wrote our doctoral dissertations under his direction. Father Spitzer also helped me to find my Jesuit vocation. I will always be in his debt.

Oremus pro invicem!

Robert McTeigue, S.J.
Sweetwater, Guerneville, California
Feast of the Chair of Saint Peter, Apostle

INDEX